HEALING THE ADDICTIONS WITHIN

BREAKING FREE: HOW TO OVERCOME ADDICTION BY HEALING YOUR INNER CHILD TRAUMA, AND REGAIN EMOTIONAL STABILITY THROUGH RECOVERY

ANNE LUNAR

Trinity Sky Publishing

To my beloved family, Alberto and Hazel.

Your unwavering love and support have been the foundation of my dreams.
This book is a tribute to the boundless inspiration you've brought into my life.

CONTENTS

Part IV
FROM ADDICT TO ADVOCATE

INTRODUCTION

It is no measure of health to be well adjusted to a profoundly sick society.
–J. Krishnamurti

If current affairs and the state of your mental and emotional well-being are anything to go by, then you may admit that life just isn't how it used to be. Society has divided and turned against itself, and now more than ever, you feel the inner calling to turn inward and redefine the meaning of your existence—to avoid becoming a radical pessimist.

However, this journey of turning inward isn't as simple as tuning out the noise and reading an empowering self-help book (perhaps 10 years ago, that is all it would've taken to reconnect to yourself).

But since your identity has become so enmeshed with this sick society—and its instant gratification that comes with the click of a button—you have developed lifestyle habits, behaviors, and beliefs that have you hooked on work, relationships, and recreational activities–pretty much anything that causes you to seek meaning outwardly.

Whether you are aware of it or not, you have become an addict—however, not in the medical sense of the word. According to the Merriam-Webster Dictionary, an addict is someone who displays

[handwritten margin note: addict - someone who displays chronic or compulsive physiological or psychological need for a habit behavior or activity.]

chronic or compulsive physiological or psychological need for a habit, behavior, or activity (2018). Due to the warped ideas and questionable norms of this individualistic and consumption-driven society, you and many others have become addicted to habits and behaviors that promise a sense of wholeness, but leave you feeling more detached from yourself.

Without even knowing it, you have created the 'addict within' which is the part of you that has been wounded by life, but searches for healing in all the wrong places. In your efforts to seek meaning, you have found solace in cheap thrills, external validation, symbols of success, or 'keeping up with the Joneses.'

This may not be where you saw your life heading, but since the addict within doesn't know how to acknowledge and heal emotional wounds or past traumas, it has succumbed to maladaptive behaviors that promote numbing out, denying reality, self-sabotage, or withdrawing from others.

Psychoanalyst and psychiatrist, Carl Jung, believed that addiction had somewhat of a positive benefit for patients. For a moment, it allowed the addict to believe they were free from the psychological distress. The 'drug of choice' per se, had psychic abilities to give the illusion of a peaceful inner life and a false sense of wholeness. Thus, it wasn't necessarily the habit or activity the addict was hooked on, but that short-lived experience of finally being healed.

The reason you may turn to substances, social media, romantic relationships, gambling, or work, as much as you do may be due to the sense of wholeness these things offer you. For a brief moment, they calm the addict within and make you feel like your life is in perfect harmony. However, as Jung pointed out, the sense of wholeness that comes with addictive behaviors is illusory, and will quickly disappear when you sober up to the reality of your life.

The addict within is something we all have. It is that wounded self that tries desperately to hide, numb, and deny the pain of yesteryears. The more successful it is at this endeavor, the more susceptible you become to developing life-threatening addictions, such as being addicted to drugs and alcohol, prescription medication, gambling, sex, shopping, or working.

To prevent having to experience life-threatening addictions, this book seeks to help you understand and respond to the addict within, so you don't have to live another year with unresolved psychological trauma, which may or may not cause significant harm to you or your livelihood.

This book is recommended for those who are already showing signs of addiction, as well as those who recognize harmful habits or beliefs they would like to address. If you are already displaying signs of addiction, there is no need to panic. Take it as your mind and body's way of bringing your attention to your inner life. Perhaps all this time you haven't paid any attention to your inner life, or the concept of your inner girl, and now you have the opportunity to learn more about this aspect of who you are. It may even be better for you to read the first part of this series, *Healing the Girl Within*, first, so you can get an in-depth understanding of who the inner girl is, and how you can respond to its needs.

Finally, this book will offer you ways of achieving what you have always wanted—a sense of wholeness—which isn't through maladaptive behaviors or anything that causes you to disconnect from self. Instead, the practical solutions you will be given encourage you to turn to lost traditions, like establishing community, finding your purpose, and connecting to spirituality. These traditions are often seen as 'alternative' in modern society, but they are still reliable ways to achieve self-actualization—the final stage on Maslow's hierarchy of needs.

It is worth emphasizing again that this book is not focused on diagnosing addiction, and the information shared with you is not a substitute for seeking medical diagnosis or advice. However, it is still important for you to know how to recognize addictive behaviors, and where they might possibly stem from, as part of the process of healing the addict within.

PART I

THE LIFE OF AN ADDICT

RECOGNIZE ADDICTION AND ADDICTIVE BEHAVIORS

There are all kinds of addicts, I guess. We all have pain. And we all look for ways
to make the pain go away.
–Sherman Alexie

DEFINING ADDICTION

Jane always had a sweet tooth. She was the kind of person to order dessert first when going to restaurants. Her friends even knew that if they wanted to butter her up before asking for favors, they had to bring her a gift basket full of candy.

After a health scare, Jane realized that she was consuming too much sugar. Following the advice of a nutritionist, she decided to go on a sugar-free diet for three months. When the three months were over, her cravings for sugar had decreased significantly, and she was able to adopt healthier eating habits moving forward.

Cynthia also grew up with a sweet tooth. Coming from a strict household, candy was used as a reward for good behavior. This is ironic since sugar is a mind and mood-altering substance that increases dopamine (the happy hormone). Cynthia knew that if she could be a 'good girl' and please her parents, she would be rewarded with pleasurable feelings.

Fast forward to 15 years later, and Cynthia found herself in a rehabilitation center for sugar addiction. Not only was she embarrassed that she was addicted to sugar (something she thought was a ridiculous idea) but she felt ashamed at her lack of self-control.

Unlike Jane, Cynthia couldn't go on a sugar-free diet and just stop consuming sugar. Even though she could see how destructive her behavior was for her health, sugar made her feel good about herself and gave her a sense of euphoria. Like any other addictive substance, it allowed her to feel free from the weight of the world and calmed the inner girl inside of her that never felt seen or accepted by her parents.

From the story of these two women, you can see what addiction is and what it isn't. Addiction isn't the same as having bad habits. Let's face it—we all have bad habits, some that we have lived with for many years, yet we are not controlled by our habits. For instance, Jane had an insatiable craving for sugar, but after confronting her habit, she was able to reduce her sugar intake.

Addiction only takes place when a bad habit becomes a go-to or default coping mechanism for dealing with psychological triggers or distress. In Cynthia's case, eating sugary desserts became her way of suppressing emotions and feeling good about herself. Over time, it became more difficult for her to control the impulse to consume sugar. This is because whenever her brain desired a pick-me-up, it immediately turned to sugar to release those happy hormones. Soon enough, consuming sugar became less about the taste for Cynthia, and more about feeding her uncontrollable impulses.

The most widespread misconception about addiction is that it is a personal choice. In Cynthia's case, one might think she chose to put the sugary desserts in her mouth. When commenting about a workaholic, one might think the individual has chosen to dedicate their entire lives to work, to their own detriment.

They might say things like, *"Why don't they just stop working if they are complaining about it so much?"* or *"They chose to make work the center of their*

4

lives." This notion that the workaholic has a choice in becoming addicted to work may even cause the observer to believe that being addicted to work is a sign of the individual's character flaw or weakness.

However, no one chooses to have an addiction—even if the addictive substance or behavior is something they once found pleasurable. In fact, one of the reasons many people deny having an addiction in the first place is due to the shame and self-blame that comes with acknowledging you have no control over your thoughts or behaviors. No one would deliberately choose to lose themselves in anything, or be driven by compulsions to the extent of causing misery for themselves and their families.

In the 1930s, researchers began studying what addiction was all about. They wanted to investigate the causes of addiction and test the hypothesis that addiction was due to a lack of willpower. Studies found that repeated performance of certain habits or behaviors led to physical changes in brain chemistry that inhibited self-control and caused uncontrollable urges. This breakthrough discovery disproved the myth that addiction is a personal choice, and many scientific associations like the National Institute on Drug Abuse (NIDA) and the American Psychiatric Association (APA) defined addiction as a brain disease or mental illness.

Substance vs. Behavioral Addiction

Many years ago, the term 'addiction' was used to refer to substance abuse, particularly the dependency on drugs, nicotine, alcohol, and prescription medication. However, behavioral scientists argued that any activity that is capable of stimulating an individual can become addictive.

This discovery expanded the definition of addiction to include any substance, behavior, or activity that created a compulsive physiological or psychological need. This meant that individuals could become addicted to everyday lifestyle habits and experiences, which induce the same 'chemical high' as substances.

To understand the similarities and differences between substance and behavioral addictions, we will need to look at each separately.

Substance Addiction

Substance addiction, also known as chemical addiction, refers to consuming certain substances that bind to receptors in your brain and change your brain chemistry. While the effects of each substance differ, what's common is how they make you feel a sense of euphoria. Your brain becomes addicted to this sense of euphoria, not necessarily the substance, and it leads you to make personal sacrifices to maintain the chemically-induced high.

Due to the nature of substance addiction and how it causes neurological changes, medical professionals have classified it as a mental illness. Substance abusers, for example, find it difficult to function in their everyday lives without their drug of choice, and prolonged usage leads to increased dosages—which makes it that much more difficult for the user to control their urges.

The list of addictive substances is extensive. In general, any substance that can alter your mood can become highly addictive. Examples of common addictive substances include:

- alcohol
- nicotine
- cocaine
- opioids (i.e. Prescription medication, like morphine, and drugs like heroin)
- amphetamines
- methamphetamines

There are also early warning signs that you can look out for that can help you determine if you have a substance abuse problem. These early signs include:

- Intense cravings that cause you to lose concentration.
- The urge to increase your dosage of the substance so you can get the same, or a better high.
- Feeling irritable or restless when you can't access the substance.
- Risky substance use, like going to work or driving while under the influence.
- Experiencing trouble managing daily tasks and responsibilities due to reoccupation with substance use.
- Experiencing conflict in relationships due to substance use.
- The inability to stop using the substance, even when you desire to stop.
- Intense withdrawal symptoms when you attempt to go cold turkey.

Behavioral Addiction

Instead of creating dependency on a substance, a behavioral addiction leads to compulsive actions that aren't related to the use of substances (although chemical and behavioral addictions often exist together).

The part of your brain that is affected by a behavioral addiction is the risk and reward system. This happens to be the same system that leads to habit formation. In other words, just as you can get easily sucked into the habit of going to the gym, it is possible to become addicted to physical exercise.

The fact that habits and addictions are formed in the same part of the brain should make you more cautious about what you do—and the intentions behind why you do certain things or act in certain ways. However, just because a behavior feels good, doesn't mean that you will become addicted to it. Acting out certain behaviors to receive a psychological reward isn't what triggers addiction. If this were the case, then you would be addicted to healthy pursuits, like spending time with family, setting and achieving goals, or practicing self-care.

What makes a behavior addictive is the power it has over you, and how it causes you to place it at the center of your life. In other words, you do not get a surge of dopamine unless you are performing that specific behavior. It becomes the only source of motivation for you to get up in the morning, and as a result, you may even notice that other areas of your life begin to suffer as a result of spending most of your time and effort on a specific behavior.

Unlike someone who is battling a chemical addiction, an individual with a behavioral addiction may find it easier to hide their destructive behaviors. This is because many of the behaviors we become addicted to are not seen as taboo in society. For example, who would stop a loved one who decided to lose weight? Isn't weight loss an acceptable, and even celebrated, activity in society? The reason for the weight loss may be due to an eating disorder, but by the time people realize what is actually happening, the person may already be addicted to restricting foods.

Thus, one might say that there are fewer social consequences when it comes to behavioral addictions than there are with chemical addictions. In fact, since our society is so sick, many media companies and mega corporations play on these behavioral addictions to pocket millions of dollars. Promoting an upsized meal to someone who is struggling with an eating disorder is not considered socially irresponsible; nor is advertising the latest cosmetic treatments to young girls who are addicted to self-enhancement products.

While the list of behavioral addictions is endless, here are a few of the common behavioral addictions many people face:

- TV and electronic devices
- gambling
- food
- work
- social media
- shopping
- sex and dating
- success (or the pursuit of success)
- health (or the pursuit of health)

Your mind and body will give you early warning signs of behavioral addiction. Some of these might include:

- Spending an excessive amount of time on the behavior.
- The uncontrollable urge to engage in the behavior, even if it interferes with your daily life or leads to negative consequences.
- Turning to the behavior whenever you want to release unwanted emotions.
- Hiding or lying about the behavior when asked about it.
- Feeling irritable, depressed, or anxious whenever you attempt to quit.

Obsession vs. Addiction

Obsessions are often confused with addictions. This is an innocent mistake since the two look very similar, and are usually experienced together. However, obsession and addictive behavior are rooted in two different things, thus making them unique experiences. *anxiety*

Obsessive behavior, for example, is rooted in fear. The cycle typically begins with a fear-based thought, then leads to feelings of anxiety, which subsequently motivate the compulsive behavior. The more you give into the fear-based thoughts, the more intense the feelings of anxiety become in the following cycles. For example, you might believe that if you don't double-check the front door five times before you sleep, you are putting your family's life in danger.

Addictive behavior, on the other hand, isn't rooted in fear but instead, in the sense of dissatisfaction, you may have with yourself or your life. You turn to substances or behaviors because they provide you with an escape from your mundane existence, or offer temporary relief from stress or unresolved trauma. As mentioned above, it is possible for obsessive and addictive behaviors to exist simultaneously, or for one to eventually trigger the other. For example, someone addicted to sports betting may become obsessed with analyzing sports or following certain sports viewing rituals. Or it can work the other way too: An individual obsessed with counting calories may later develop an eating disorder.

Or even worse, consider the athlete who is injured and forced to sit out of games. Their doctor prescribed pain pills to generate more comfort during healing. The athlete notices that when they take the pills, they don't feel anything. They quickly become addicted to pills to the point of not being able to function, or even play the game they love without them. Just like that the coping mechanism has become an addiction.

Moreover, researchers have found that people who have an obsessive or compulsive personality trait are more susceptible to developing an addiction. The addiction may start off as a compulsion to either use a substance or control certain behaviors using substances. For example, someone who is an obsessive thinker may turn to anxiety drugs like benzodiazepines to calm their mind. However, misusing this kind of drug can lead to addiction.

RED FLAGS CHECKLIST

Since no one chooses addiction, it is extremely important to be vigilant of signs of addiction during the onset. This will give you the opportunity to seek professional help and reverse the early mental, physical, and psychological effects of addiction.

Below is a checklist of red flags to be on the lookout for, related to your physical and mental health, as well as addict behaviors you may have adopted. Please note that these red flags may be caused by various types of addictions, and are not exclusive to drug and alcohol addiction.

Lastly, these red flags are not diagnostic tools, but rather signs that may indicate a much deeper problem.

If you can identify with many of these red flags, consider seeking medical attention immediately.

Physical Red Flags		
Common Signs	Yes	No
Impaired physical coordination		
Sleepiness during the day		
Red eyes		
Slowed or slurred speech		
Jumpiness or rapid speech		
Physical signs of self-neglect, such as poor hygiene		
Lip and finger burns		

Mental/Emotional Red Flags		
Common Signs	Yes	No
Anxiety		
Depression		
Confusion		
Insomnia		
Memory loss or forgetfulness		
Illogical thinking		
Frequent mood swings		
Poor emotional regulation		

Behavioral Red Flags		
Common Signs	Yes	No
Unusual or erratic behavior		
Poor decision-making		
Loss of interest in daily tasks or social activities		
Defensiveness when the topic of addiction is brought up		
Impulsiveness		
Financial problems		
Getting in trouble with law enforcement		
Blaming others, or rationalizing behavior		

2

ADDICTION AND ITS HOLD ON THE MIND, AND BODY

Most substance-addicted people are also addicted to thinking, meaning they have a compulsive and unhealthy relationship with their own thinking.
–David Foster Wallace

ESCAPING REALITY AND CHASING ILLUSIONS

You were born with a deep sense of freedom ingrained in your mind. As a young child, you were unapologetic about how you expressed your individuality–even if it brought about roaring laughter from the adults around you.

However, as you became older, you were conditioned to behave according to the dictates of your family, school, and community. The same expressive behaviors that used to make adults laugh, soon caused them to look upon you with judgment. The message you got from early social conditioning was clear: *Either act right or be condemned.*

Fast forward many years later into your adult life. You are still doing everything you can to maintain your place on the totem pole of modern society. Even though you have gained more independence now than when you were a child, there is still a part of you that seeks validation from others.

The reason I bring up social conditioning and how it has shaped who you are is so that you can understand why some people desire to escape from reality. The societal pressure imposed on individuals to behave a certain way, adopt certain ideals, and aim for certain goals is enough to make anyone feel tired, anxious, or depressed.

Whether you log into social media, turn on the radio, or catch up with friends, you are constantly reminded of how fast life is moving and how slowly you are lagging behind. And if it isn't society reminding you of personal inadequacies, then it is your mind causing you to turn against yourself, and ultimately reject your own reality.

An addict is an individual, like you and me, who has reached a point where they have rejected reality. You can imagine how much pain the addict must experience for them to disconnect from everything and everyone, and pick up their drug or behavior of choice. Through their actions, they replace one tyrant—the cutthroat society —with another tyrant—the ruthless mind.

On the surface, this seems like a good deal since the mind allows plenty of opportunities for escapism and entertaining illusions. But eventually, these illusions start to feel more real than reality itself. In other words, an addict is trapped in the illusions they have created in their minds, which makes them lose touch with reality.

The Role of the Brain in Chasing Illusions

You would never think that your own brain would sell you out to addiction, but it can. Your brain is a three-pound mass of matter that governs all mind and body activity. If your body was a house, your brain would be the main switchboard that powers everything inside. Not only does your brain control basic functions, such as walking, eating, or breathing, but it also controls cognitive and psychological functions, such as decision-making, emotional regulation, or interpreting experiences.

In order to send and receive signals from various parts of the body, your brain relies on billions of cells known as neurons. Neurons are organized in circuits and networks, so they can better control the flow and processing of different types of information. Networks of neurons send and receive messages to each other, and to different parts of the brain and body.

Chemical and behavioral addiction affects brain chemistry, which is the natural chemical balance in your brain that is necessary to carry out daily functions. Once this natural balance is altered, it causes you to think and behave compulsively. Below is a brief explanation of the different parts of the brain affected by addiction and the consequences thereof:

1. Basal Ganglia

The basal ganglia is the part of the brain responsible for the planning of movement, memory, motivation, and reward processing. It plays a significant role in inducing pleasurable feelings from activities like sex, eating, or socializing, and can also help you learn habits and routines.

When you become dependent on a substance or behavior, the basal ganglia becomes hyperactive, producing the 'high' that many become addicted to. However, with repeated stimulation of the basal ganglia, the circuit adapts to the euphoric feeling induced by the substance or behavior, and it becomes difficult to feel a sense of pleasure from anything else besides the drug or behavior of choice.

2. Extended Amygdala *fear response / stress response*

The extended amygdala is the part of the brain that plays a role in orchestrating fear or anxiety as a response to stimuli, and can lead to the development of anxiety, depression, or substance abuse. When you attempt to go cold turkey and quit using the drug of choice (or performing the compulsive behavior), the extended amygdala creates withdrawal symptoms characterized by feelings of stress, anxiety, and irritability.

These unpleasurable symptoms are what motivate you to pick up the drug or behavior again. Over time, the extended amygdala becomes ~~~~~~~~~~~~ sensitive, which means you feel highly stressed or anxious when you are not engaging with your addiction. After a while, your primary motivation for using the drug (or performing the behavior) is to reduce your feelings of stress or anxiety, rather than chasing a high.

3. Prefrontal Cortex

The prefrontal cortex is the part of the brain responsible for your thoughts, emotions, planning and problem-solving abilities, and self-control. When your brain releases too much dopamine (triggered by a compulsive behavior or substance), it causes a chemical imbalance in the prefrontal cortex. This can lead to a decrease in awareness and cognitive function, as well as poor emotional regulation and impulse control.

Besides changing brain chemistry, addiction can also be triggered by the release of too much dopamine. In healthy dosages, dopamine is good for mental health and well-being because it makes you feel positive about life. However, as the saying goes, "Too much of a good thing is never good" (Farlex Dictionary of Idioms, 2015).

There are many pleasurable activities and behaviors that can cause you to become hooked on dopamine. Your brain begins to crave the sense of reward induced by performing these activities, even if they are indulgent activities like eating a whole tub of ice cream.

The high levels of dopamine released in certain parts of your brain can make you feel energetic, competitive, aggressive, and have poor impulse control. However, the intense euphoria released when taking substances or performing compulsive behaviors is enough to make your brain seek addictive behaviors above healthier activities.

Scientists have studied why addictive substances and behaviors release more dopamine than non-addictive substances and behaviors. They have found that since addictive substances and behaviors produce too much dopamine, the brain—in an attempt to regulate the reward circuit—will reduce the number of neurons that can receive pleasure signals. As a result, it becomes more difficult to experience a sense of satisfaction from any other stimulating and pleasurable activity.

Over time, even the addictive behavior starts to make you feel indifferent, even though at this stage you cannot control the impulse to perform it. This is why you may end up losing motivation and feeling depressed, since you are unable to derive pleasure from naturally rewarding experiences, like being with family or pursuing meaningful goals. The only way you can feel any sense of pleasure—regardless of how small it can be—is when you are engaging in your addiction, which creates a vicious cycle.

EMOTIONAL REGULATION AND ADDICTION

We have discussed how chasing the illusions of the mind and changes in brain chemistry can lead to addiction. However, there are a myriad of other factors that may trigger addiction. In this section, we will speak about how poor emotional regulation and unresolved trauma play a role in developing an addiction.

In psychology, emotional regulation refers to how you influence which emotions you have, how you have them, and when it is most appropriate. No one is born knowing how to respond to circumstances with the most appropriate emotions, thus this skill is often learned through early childhood experiences and developed over time.

Society expects you to have already learned how to regulate your emotions by the time you reach adult status. However, learning emotional regulation skills is not a rite of passage. While physical maturity comes with age, emotional regulation is developed when you are able to:

- Modify the intensity, duration, range, and recovery from emotional experiences.
- Organize your life in a way that increases the probability of positive experiences.
- Regulate and make changes to your environment to change its effects on your emotional experiences.

- Adjust how you perceive or interpret unavoidable situations.
- Weigh the consequences of various behavioral reactions, and choose adaptive coping strategies to positively alter your moods.

The lack of emotional regulation skills is what makes it difficult for you to manage your moods or modify how you perceive, and subsequently, respond to emotional experiences. It can make facing emotional triggers feel too threatening, and lead to maladaptive coping strategies, such as emotional withdrawal, avoidance, mental dissociation, or defensiveness.

If you are someone who finds it difficult to regulate their emotions, turning to addictive substances or behaviors can seem like the best way to manage how you feel, and what you feel. For instance, instead of accepting the reality of a stressful job and working through those emotions, you might decide to turn to your love for shopping as a gateway to happiness. This is because addictive behaviors, especially during the early stages, can increase pleasurable feelings while decreasing stress and anxiety. You might tell yourself, "I feel stressed about work, so I will treat myself to a new pair of shoes."

Unresolved Trauma and Addiction

What makes strong emotions difficult to manage is due to what they might be masking. When you see someone who is addicted to social media fighting their urge to go online, what you are actually witnessing is a person who is refusing to feed into their addiction to social validation. They may or may not realize that their need to keep track of 'likes' and 'shares' is rooted in deeper self-esteem issues caused by bullying during their early years of life.

Traumatic events shape who you are. They influence how you see yourself and others, and what you choose to believe about your life situation. The stress triggered during a life-threatening event or period affects not only your sense of safety but can cause the collapse of your entire belief system. It can feel like having your life reset, and now you are left to redefine, re-learn, and re-create who you are.

The stress of having to rebuild your life following a traumatic event or period is enough to cause some to turn to addictive substances or behaviors. This is especially true when the survivor is not ready to undergo the process of healing. It can feel less emotionally taxing to self-medicate or indulge in risky behaviors as a way to cope with their experiences.

Drugs and alcohol, in particular, are known to ease some of the symptoms associated with post-traumatic stress disorder (PTSD), such as insomnia, irritability, social withdrawal, and depression. Even though the survivor's intention is never to develop an addiction, trying to 'cure' trauma with substances can lead to substance dependence and abuse.

By looking back at how addictive substances and behaviors affect the brain, you can understand why anyone who was constantly flooded with feelings of guilt, shame, denial, or anxiety would turn to cravings or compulsions as a source of comfort. The temporary relief found in addictive substances or behaviors becomes their hope of healing. In that state of euphoria, driven by a dopamine rush, the survivor no longer feels endangered by their environment. As we know, their sense of happiness or hopefulness is illusory and even though it feels real, it doesn't change the painful reality that awaits once the high wears off.

Before we move on to the next section where we will look deeper into the 'addict within,' take a moment to review the last two chapters, and then reflect on how your life experiences have impacted your mind and body. Think about the kinds of coping strategies you have turned to during difficult moments in the past, and the impact of these strategies on your self-esteem, lifestyle choices, and relationships with others.

PART II

THE ADDICT WITHIN

3

SELF-CONCEPT AND HEALING THE ADDICT WITHIN

We frantically expend our lives attempting to be what we think we should be, rather than being who we are. And if we would just settle into ourselves, we would soon discover that that is who we should have been all along.
–Craig D. Lounsbrough

WHO IS THE 'ADDICT WITHIN?'

In the first part of the book, we defined addiction and looked at how it affects the brain and body. We also got to step into the shoes of an addict and understand some of the triggers that lead to the development of an addiction.

This second part of the book moves away from discussing the reality of being an addict, and instead, it explores the psychological factors that would cause someone to fall victim to an addiction. In other words, we will look at some of the early childhood experiences, emotional wounds, and traumas that lead to maladaptive behaviors and self-abandonment in adulthood.

When you experience trauma, neglect, or loss in childhood, it creates what is known as the 'split self.' The split self refers to the different sides of you that emerge as a way to cope or recover from

PTSD. For example, one part of you might feel unlovable, another part of you might overcompensate by being overly confident and sociable, while another part might desire to heal and freely express who you are.

Splitting is a psychological coping mechanism that protects your inner life from being completely damaged by trauma. Your mind creates different personas that can shield it from various attacks caused by painful life experiences. These personas are what helped you bounce back from one struggle after the next as a young child–when survival was your main priority.

Nevertheless, the split self is also what breeds the addict within—the part of you that never fully recovers from pain, and always seeks to avoid, numb, or deny its existence. Later on in life, it is this part of you that makes you vulnerable to chemical and behavioral addictions, and making it even harder to address the damage caused by trauma.

The 'addict within' feels ashamed about the devastating experiences of the past and tries by all means to reject the part of you that went through those experiences. Think of the addict within as that highly critical and ruthless part of you that has no sympathy for all the suffering you have endured, but instead reminds you to keep your past a secret, or just suck it up and continue living.

For example, if you grew up in a household where expressing anger was seen as taboo, you may have learned to hide your anger better, rather than processing and working through it. Since the anger was split off, but remained a very real part of you, it may have emerged later on in life through behavioral issues, insecurities, or addiction. Since the addict within seeks to hide trauma under the rug, it carries with it a lot of shame, and with shame comes denial.

To summarize who the addict within is, we can say that it is that part of you that has been hurt in the past but never given yourself the opportunity to heal. Instead of dealing with past traumas head-on, you felt it was better to simply move on, suck it up, and avoid pitying yourself. However, denying your pain hasn't caused it to miraculously disappear, but instead has made you turn to maladaptive behaviors and risky activities as a way to keep the pain bottled up inside.

The reason we call this part of you the 'addict within' is because, similar to an addict, it believes that disconnecting from the wounded parts of yourself somehow makes them disappear. However, we know that this isn't true. Disconnecting from the wounded parts of yourself simply prolongs the healing process and puts you at risk of developing severe mental and emotional issues.

Throughout the rest of the chapter, we will look at how the addict within develops as a result of low self-esteem, attachment during early childhood development, and cultural identity and norms. We will also look at how all of these factors lead to emotional wounds that ultimately cause the splitting to take place.

DEFINE WHO YOU ARE

Self-concept is the idea you have about who you are. It is how you would describe yourself to a stranger, the way you would solve problems or understand certain situations, or how you would interact with others.

Your self-concept is also what helps you define your core values, beliefs, and personality. It is the sum of your strengths and weaknesses, skills, and natural abilities. As much as self-concept is about how you define yourself, it isn't formed by your opinions or perceptions only. The society you grew up in, friends and family who played a major role in your upbringing, and the life experiences you have overcome, all form part of how you define who you are.

American psychologist, Carl Rogers, believed that your self-concept was made of three components (Cherry, 2022):

- **Ideal self:** The person you aspire to become, who has all of the qualities you are either working on or would like to someday possess. It is the version of you that appears in dreams or visions of the future.
- **Self-image:** The person you identify as at this present moment, including how you perceive your personality, social roles, and physical characteristics.

- **Self-esteem:** How much value you see in yourself and how you believe you compare to others. Your self-esteem also helps you define your strengths, work on your weaknesses, and seek to become a better version of yourself.

Your self-concept isn't always representative of reality. In other words, there are instances where how you see yourself and how others see you are incongruent. Or the value you believe you hold is mismatched from the value you actually contribute to those around you. When there is a misalignment between the perception and reality of who you are, it can negatively impact your self-esteem.

Having low self-esteem can make you more sensitive to difficulties in life, such as being rejected by a loved one, or criticized about who you are. Someone with high self-esteem may still be hurt by these experiences, but they are able to modify negative experiences through the lens of their positive self-image. In other words, negative life experiences are less likely to leave behind emotional wounds or cause you to ruminate over what was said when your self-esteem is high.

Having high self-esteem further reduces the need to split. Since you have a greater acceptance of who you are, despite what others might say or think, you can embrace your strengths and weaknesses. Even when you make mistakes, you are less likely to walk around feeling ashamed of yourself. Instead, you realize that you are not perfect, nor do you feel the pressure to be. And while there are some aspects of your personality you can improve on, there is no part of you that you would reject or deem as unlovable or inappropriate.

Here are a few common signs that you may have a low self-esteem:

- You don't trust yourself to make the best decisions concerning your life.
- You feel like you have little control over what happens to you, due to the lack of confidence to create the positive changes you desire in your life.
- You feel powerless to fix your own problems, and often envy others who are able to get themselves out of difficult life

situations.

- You perceive yourself as being lesser than others and often compare yourself unfavorably to other people's achievements.
- You struggle to ask for what you need because a part of you believes you don't deserve to have your needs met.
- You worry often about making the wrong choices, and how humiliating it will be when your plans don't work out accordingly.
- You are suspicious of compliments and positive feedback, especially when they don't align with what you believe about yourself.

Self-Concept and Early Childhood Attachment

Attachment theory, developed by psychologist Mary Ainsworth and psychiatrist John Bowlby, argues that the manner in which a child interacts with their caregiver, in particular their parents, is an indicator of the child's confidence later in life (Florida Tech, 2018). Moreover, since the parent-child attachment is the first relationship the child will experience, it sets the tone for how the child will interact and form relationships with others.

Children don't get to choose which families they are born into. Ideally, we hope that all children are raised by conscious parents in a safe and nurturing home environment. But this isn't always the case.

Unfortunately, many children are raised in dysfunctional home environments where one or both parents are either physically absent, neglectful, or emotionally unavailable. Having disconnected parents doesn't stop children from forming attachments because as healthy or unhealthy as their parents are, they depend on them for survival.

Infants start to form attachments with a single caregiver from 7—9 months old, and by 10 months old, they have formed multiple attachments with different caregivers, such as their parents, grandparents, and non-family caregivers. What drives early childhood attachments is the level of responsiveness of caregivers to children's emotional needs and bids. For example, a child might look out for a parent's smile as a sign of reassurance, or a desire to be held when crying as a sign of protection. Thus, the more responsive a caregiver is, the healthier and stronger their attachment becomes with the child.

The four attachment styles describe four types of relationships children can form with parents. Depending on the attachment style, children learn what is and isn't acceptable when relating with others. Remember, the attachments formed in these primary relationships are what inform how children relate with others—and most importantly how they build their self-concept. Below is a brief explanation of each attachment style:

- **Anxious attachment:** An insecure attachment style where the child worries about the possibility of being abandoned by their parents. This causes them to constantly seek validation from their parents, which could manifest as needy or clingy behavior.
- **Avoidant attachment:** Another insecure attachment style that is characterized by the fear of intimacy. A child with this type of attachment may be raised by emotionally unavailable parents, and has learned to self-soothe and rely on themselves from a very young age.
- **Fearful-avoidant attachment:** This is a combination of the anxious and avoidant attachment styles, and usually occurs when a child has been exposed to abuse or trauma. The child desires intimacy with their parents but also avoids it at all costs. And even though they may be feeling deeply, the child struggles to express or regulate their emotions.
- **Secure attachment:** A secure attachment style where the child feels safe to bond with their parents, trust that their needs will be met, and build intimacy with ease. Parents are usually reassuring through verbal and non-verbal gestures, which makes the child feel comfortable loving and accepting love.

Looking at the four attachment styles above, which one do you resonate with most? It is very likely that the attachment style you resonate with most is a mirror of the same type of attachment you had growing up with your parents. And even more, this attachment style may very well be how you relate with others in your adult relationships.

Your attachment style may have also played a role in how you developed your self-concept. For instance, if you had a secure attachment with your parents, you may have grown up feeling confident in who you are, due to receiving a lot of reassurance at home. This may have encouraged you to perform well at school, set meaningful goals for yourself, and have a greater ability to work and collaborate with others.

In contrast, if you had an insecure attachment with your parents, you may have grown up doubting your capabilities, being needy of others, displaying clingy or withdrawn behavior, or struggling to cope with stress and anxiety. This could have been because, for the most part, you were forced to raise yourself and learned how to deal with emotional distress on your own, rather than having your parents model healthy coping skills, or teach you emotional regulation skills.

If you grew up with insecure attachment, it is also likely that you found ways to get your parents' attention through performing maladaptive behaviors. For example, being a 'good girl' and hiding your distress may have been one way of pleasing a hot-tempered parent. It may have also made you feel less guilty for your parent's emotional outbursts. Later on in life, internalizing your feelings may have led to anxiety, difficulty setting boundaries or communicating your needs, and other poor coping strategies.

Self-Concept and Cultural Identity

Who you are today is shaped by your early childhood attachment with your parents, but it is also informed by your cultural upbringing. We can define culture as the learned and shared values, beliefs, attitudes, and behaviors from socializing institutions, such as your family, school, peers, and the media.

Your cultural identity is, therefore, the self that was constructed as a result of growing up with particular family dynamics, living in a particular neighborhood, going to a particular school, and being influenced by particular friends and media. Since culture creates patterns of beliefs and behaviors, there will be noticeable similarities between you and those who were exposed to the same culture. In fact, you are more likely to share similar beliefs about what is wrong or right, desirable or undesirable with members of your culture, rather than individuals from a different cultural group.

It is important to think about who you are from a cultural perspective, as this can explain why you have adopted certain beliefs, or why you have deemed certain behaviors acceptable or unacceptable. For example, according to the American Academy of Child and Adolescent Psychiatry, children of alcoholics are four times more likely to become alcoholics later in life than other children (AACAP, 2019). Moreover, due to the exposure to substance abuse, children of alcoholics are more likely to experience some other form of abuse or neglect at home.

Besides influencing your behaviors, your culture can also influence how you perceive yourself. For instance, it is common for families, schools, churches, or other social institutions to assign labels to individuals as a way of describing who they are. Even though each individual is unique, society tends to see people in general terms, like male or female, single or married, rich or poor, attractive or unattractive.

Assigning individuals labels is also another way for society to reinforce cultural values, beliefs, and norms. For example, it is easier to spread the belief that men are supposed to be providers and women nurturers, instead of making exceptions for each man and each woman. And the more entrenched these kinds of beliefs are in a community, the harder it becomes for the community to see past the labels.

Take a moment and think about the unconscious labels you have ascribed to yourself based on the family and community you grew up in. These could be labels based on race, gender, sexuality, economic class, religion, and so on. You may have also received labels based on your physical appearance, disabilities, or personality. Consider how these labels have made it difficult for you to accept who you genuinely are.

Next, listen carefully to the small voice inside your head–the voice that makes ongoing commentary about your life. Looking back at your cultural upbringing, whose voice does it most sound like? Is it the voice of your parents? School teacher? Or childhood bullies?

Oftentimes, your self-talk comes from patterns of acceptable forms of communication during your upbringing. For instance, if you grew accustomed to hearing that you were a failure from a critical school teacher, your mind recorded those painful words and continued to replay them long after they had been spoken. This may have caused you to assign yourself the label of 'failure,' even though it wasn't a true reflection of your capabilities.

Not only does your mind record words and phrases, but it can also memorize tone and the way certain beliefs made you feel. For instance, as an adult, you are more likely to remember if your parents' values and beliefs made you feel loved, accepted, and respected, even if you don't recall what those values and beliefs were.

WHEN TO HEAL THE ADDICT WITHIN

There is no escaping the addict within because none of us can escape experiencing trauma at some stage in our lives. However, just as much as you can heal from trauma, you can also heal the addict within.

In other words, having low self-esteem, coming from a difficult family background, or being burdened by what others think about you, don't need to become how you live the rest of your life.

You don't have to spend the rest of your adult years shutting down whenever you feel emotionally triggered, or continue to walk through life with your head hanging in shame. Moreover, the feelings of rejection, abandonment, or embarrassment that sum up the relationships with your early childhood caregivers, don't have to be recurring themes in your adult relationships, because once you identify the addict within, you can change how you respond to, and work through emotional distress.

Healing the addict within ought to be a process that you go through at least once in your lifetime, regardless of whether you have any known addictions or not. It ought to be the official rite of passage into adulthood, where you vow to close the chapters of your past by making peace with wounded parts of yourself. It is through healing the addict within that you can begin to integrate your split selves and finally see yourself as being a whole and lovable individual.

You can delay the process of healing the addict within, although bear in mind that the longer you leave your emotional wounds to fester, the more vulnerable you become to physical and mental illness, including falling prey to addictions of all kinds. Below are a few behavioral signs that will prove that it is time to heal the addict within:

- **Rigidity:** You are uptight and inflexible about your work and life routines. This is due to operating from a place of fear (being worried that something bad will happen if you embrace change), rather than love.
- **Anger:** You experience sudden bouts of uncontrollable anger, even when the situation doesn't call for it. Your strong feelings of anger flow from one relationship or interaction to another, and this can at times leave you feeling embarrassed.
- **Avoidance:** When faced with a difficult situation, you tend to run away or ignore others. You may also see matters as either being black or white, which causes you to enter prolonged periods of isolation when you feel wronged.
- **Compliance:** If you grew up with people-pleasing tendencies, you may be uncomfortable drawing boundaries with others or expressing your needs. This can lead to complying with others' demands, even when they are unfavorable to you.

- **Denial:** You deny the reality of your life situation, or the need for healing, intimacy, self-care, or any other form of love you can give to yourself or others. You may also struggle to open up to others about your life because there are still parts of you that you cannot accept.
- **Emotional instability:** Your mood changes can be triggered by minor changes to your work or personal life. Sometimes, you oscillate between two extremes (i.e. feeling on top of the world, then feeling like the world is on top of you), which can make it difficult to maintain stable moods.

When you spot the above signs within yourself, it can signal time to heal the addict within. However, another way to know when to heal the addict within is to reflect on your life and ask these questions: *Do I often behave in ways to feel accepted by others in the world? And are my everyday actions natural expressions of who I am, or rather behaviors I have learned out of necessity?*

If you have reached the stage in life where you are ready to heal the addict within, then the best approach would be to reconnect with your inner girl—the younger version of you that was physically, mentally, and emotionally wounded from past trauma.

PART III

RECONNECT TO YOUR INNER GIRL

4

WHAT IS YOUR INNER GIRL SAYING?

The voice I finally heard that day was my own—the girl I'd locked away at ten years old, the girl I was before the world told me who to be—and she said: Here I am. I'm taking over now.
–Glennon Doyle

GET TO KNOW YOUR INNER GIRL

If you have read the first book in this series, *Healing the Girl Within*, you will be familiar with who the inner girl is. This chapter seeks to introduce the inner girl to readers who may have not heard about the concept before.

First and foremost, the inner girl should not be seen as synonymous with immaturity or childishness. There is no denying that you have grown up and have outgrown your childish ways. And as an adult, you have a deeper understanding of life and can process information, or formulate opinions and beliefs, at a greater capacity than a child.

Instead, the inner girl should be seen as the personification of your subconscious mind; the eternal part of you that has witnessed your development since you were an infant. Perhaps, we refer to it as a child because it is the embodiment of innocence and the essence of who you are. There is no masking, hiding, or faking when it comes to your inner girl. She is inspired by all things and seeks to experience all things. When she is healed, she can help you connect to your heart's desires, open your heart to love, and live without any inhibitions.

Secondly, the inner girl should not be used as an excuse for not taking responsibility for your life or your healing journey. As mentioned in the previous chapter, it is very rare to find an adult who has not experienced any form of trauma in the past. Whether it was pain you inflicted or pain that was inflicted on you, there are wounds that you carry and need to address in order to live a peaceful life. The cries of your inner girl should be seen as signs that you have emotional issues to resolve, rather than being seen as a justification for acting out maladaptive behaviors.

There is no memory or experience your inner girl doesn't remember, including those memories that have been pushed down deep into your subconscious mind. Your inner girl remembers the smell of baked bread coming from grandma's kitchen, and how adored you felt when she would cut you a generous slice. She remembers your childhood home and that secret room you would escape to hide whenever your parents got into an argument. She also remembers that gut-wrenching feeling of having your first breakup, and the famous last words from your ex, "I never want to see you again!"

Since your inner girl embodies and reflects the sum of your past experiences, it would be wrong for us to depict her as a saint or a monster. She is neither completely good nor is she completely bad. All she does is reflect your experiences back to you, and remind you of unresolved trauma.

While many people cannot hear the voice of their inner girl, they can see the manifestations of unresolved trauma through various coping strategies, lifestyle choices, and behaviors. For example, Amber grew up with a mentally ill mother who left her in charge of taking care of the household. At the age of 10, Amber was handling the household bills and assuming most of the household chores, including preparing dinner when she got home from school. Not only was being a caregiver for her mother traumatic but so was having to assume adult responsibilities at such a tender age.

Through her traumatic childhood, the addict within was being created. Amber became a highly independent and avoidant adult. She only felt useful when she was working or taking care of others, but would feel uncomfortable when others attempted to get close to her and show affection. Eventually, Amber reached her breaking point when she was admitted to the hospital for dehydration and burnout. During a counseling session, she was told she had become a workaholic. The counselor advised that she take a break from work and focus on reconnecting with her inner girl.

During her month-long break, Amber was able to enjoy quiet times where she would journal or meditate. She spent a lot of her time reflecting on her childhood and seeking to reconnect with her inner girl. As she wrote down how she felt being a 10-year caregiver, the ink on the pages was smudged with tears. Never before had she taken the time to acknowledge what her younger self went through, and how her upbringing impacted who she would later become.

She felt a sense of relief being able to validate feelings that had been forgotten for so many years. Knowing that her workaholism stemmed from early childhood experiences, she was able to set better work boundaries and invest in other aspects of her life that she had denied for years, such as the need for intimacy and closeness.

The Wounded Inner Girl

It is common for individuals to have a wounded inner girl due to past trauma. When the wounded inner girl is triggered, it is similar to witnessing a child having a full-blown meltdown. In that state of emotional distress, there seems to be nothing that can soothe the frustrated child, and after hours of uncontrollable wailing, the storm is over—but only until the next emotionally triggering experience.

When your inner girl is wounded, life can feel like a constant uphill battle. You might try by all means to live well, eat right, and stay connected with loved ones, but your unstable inner life throws curve balls several times a day, or week, that knock you off balance.

Your wounded inner girl is extremely sensitive to negative stimuli. This is because the build-up of psychological trauma over the years has caused you to become hyper-alert to unpleasant situations. Even with the slightest of inconveniences, your body reacts as though you were in a life-threatening situation, and soon enough, stress and anxiety ensue.

It can be exhausting having to put out metaphoric fires each day, or experience extreme shifts in your moods, when small changes occur in your environment. You might wake up every morning feeling on top of the world, but as the evening draws near, you are tired, depressed, and want nothing more than to isolate yourself from everything and everyone.

A wounded inner girl may be yearning for emotional needs that were not met in the past. For example, your wounded inner girl may be yearning for a sense of emotional security, something you may not have received from your parents. As much as you can try to fill this void with other things like seeking a romantic relationship, you are the only person who can bring yourself closure.

In other words, your wounded inner girl is not asking you to find people, places, or things that can bring emotional security, but instead she is asking you to find ways of making yourself feel emotionally safe. One way of doing this would be to set healthy boundaries with others, learn how to say 'no' without feeling guilty, and learn to prioritize self-care and activities that make you feel whole.

It can be both a terrifying and liberating realization to know that you are the only person who can heal the wounded inner girl. There is no superhero that will miraculously appear in your life to wipe all of the suffering away. Instead, you are the superhero or heroine that your inner girl has been waiting for all these years!

There are several ways you can identify a wounded inner girl. The first is to reflect on the childhood messages (both verbal and non-verbal) that you received from your caregivers, peers, or other members of your community. These messages often conveyed certain emotions, like a sense of guilt or disappointment, or they implied certain beliefs, like not being good enough. They may have also unconsciously taught you what's acceptable or unacceptable. For example, through childhood messages you received, you might have carried the belief that:

- Your opinions are invalid.
- Strong emotions are a sign of weakness.
- Expressing who you are makes you unlikable.
- You are not allowed to have too much fun.
- Speaking up can get you punished.
- Your caregivers are always right and you are always wrong.
- Public displays of affection are inappropriate or embarrassing.

You can also identify a wounded inner girl by the three types of trauma that many children experience: physical, emotional, and psychological neglect. Let's take a closer look at these three types of trauma and the injury they can cause later on in adulthood.

1. Physical Neglect

A sense of physical safety and nourishment is essential for human beings to thrive, especially young children who depend on others for their sense of safety and survival. When a child experiences physical neglect, they may be restricted essential needs like food, water, and proper housing, or they may be exposed to physical or sexual abuse. If this type of trauma isn't addressed, it can manifest in the following ways in adulthood:

- Low self-esteem
- Self-harm
- Eating disorders
- Addictions
- Sexual dysfunction

- Violent behavior

2. Emotional Neglect

This type of trauma occurs when caregivers are emotionally unavailable to respond to their children's emotional needs. A child feeling emotionally neglected may develop insecurities and have difficulty forming healthy relationships with others. If this type of trauma isn't addressed, it can manifest in the following ways in adulthood:

- Repressing emotions
- Anxiety
- Depression
- Low self-worth
- Ignoring one's emotional needs
- Being uncomfortable with intimacy
- Clinginess or neediness

3. Psychological Neglect

This type of trauma affects the child's psyche. It often develops when caregivers fail to validate their children, listen and respond to their needs, or accept them for who they are. In most cases, caregivers project their own psychological disorders onto their children and may resort to gaslighting, manipulation, shaming, or threatening their children as a way to gain control over them. If left unaddressed, this type of trauma can manifest in the following ways in adulthood:

- Anger and resentment
- Mental disorders
- Addictions
- Physical illness
- Difficult forming healthy relationships
- Low self-esteem and low self-worth

As you can see, the injury that you endured as a child was also endured by your inner girl. You may have forgotten most of the devastating memories of the past, but your inner girl hasn't been able to let go of them—at least not without healing first. Besides developing the addict within, here are a few more signs that you have a wounded inner girl:

- Extreme hoarder
- Perfectionist
- People-pleaser
- Malignant shame
- Body issues
- Procrastination
- Negative self-talk
- Overthinking
- Self-sabotage and obsessive behaviors
- Fear of letting go of people or possessions
- Feeling distrustful of others
- Avoid confrontation at all cost
- Fear of rejection or failure

If you can identify any of these signs in your behaviors (or any of the signs of an addict within), then you may be living with a wounded inner girl.

INNER GIRL ARCHETYPES

Carl Jung was the first person to coin the term 'inner girl.' It was one of the many divine child archetypes he discovered. Archetypes are the subconscious models of human behavior and personalities that are only obvious when we become conscious of them. On an unconscious level, archetypes influence how individuals see the world and how they relate to others.

Many years after Jung's discovery, psychologist Nicole LePera discovered seven sub-archetypes within the inner girl archetype (Adey,

2022). These seven archetypes describe ways in which the inner girl may influence adult behavior and motivations. Most of the time, each adult's display of their inner girl will look different, depending on their unique childhood experiences and cultural background.

These archetypes may not even be something that individuals are aware of, unless they are aware of how their past might continue to impact who they are and motivation behind their behaviors. Below is a list of the seven inner girl archetypes and the associated beliefs they come with:

1. The Caretaker/Self-Sacrificing Type

The caretaker prioritizes the well-being of those around them, more than their own well-being. They might appear overly concerned about others and usually derive their sense of self-worth by being helpful and sacrificing their own needs to appease others. At an early age, this individual may have been responsible for providing care to a mentally ill caregiver, or alternatively, they lack the unconditional love and acceptance from emotionally available parents.

Associated belief: "The only way to receive love is to cater to the needs of others."

2. The Overachiever/Ambitious Type

The overachiever ties their sense of self-worth with their performance. They believe that by excelling in various aspects of their life, they will finally feel accepted by others. Failure or rejection usually triggers a sense of shame and guilt due to the constant pressure they apply on themselves to succeed. As a child, the overachiever may have grown up in a family with controlling or highly critical parents. Alternatively, the overachiever may have grown up with absent parents, and the best way to get their attention was to achieve extreme measures of success.

Associated belief: "I am as good as my last performance."

3. The Underachiever/Rebel Type

The underachiever may have been a child overachiever who was never given the validation they needed for their high performance. As an adult, they have become somewhat cynical of success or standing out from the crowd, and prefer to do just enough so that they are never in the spotlight. They abhor competing with others, even though they are competitive by nature, and similar to the over-achiever, they are extremely afraid of failure or criticism from others.

Associated belief: "I am not good enough to be praised or seen by others."

4. The Rescuer/Protective Type

The rescuer is always attempting to help, educate, or save others. They believe that due to their life experiences, skills, and natural abilities, they are able to inspire change in others. Similar to the caretaker, their sense of self-worth is derived from feeling needed by others. As an adult, the rescuer is likely to fall into codependent relationships with people they believe cannot cope without them. This is usually an overcompensation for early childhood experiences where they felt neglected or helpless in their relationship with their emotionally unstable or strict parents.

Associated belief: "I have to take care of others because I am responsible for them."

5. The Eternal Child/Life of the Party Type

The eternal child displays a fun and sociable personality. They avoid feeling any kind of negative emotion or being involved in conflict of any sorts. All they want is to spend the rest of their life having fun and gathering positive experiences with others. As a child, the eternal child may have been reprimanded for showing strong emotions, such as anger, and therefore, learned to mask unpleasant emotions. They may have also been rejected for expressing their true self and decided to show up as a lovable and non-threatening individual instead.

Associated belief: "I will be accepted by others when I make them feel good and spread positivity."

6. The Yes Person/People-Pleasing Type

The yes person is similar to the caretaker, as both are willing to sacrifice their own needs for the needs of others. However, what motivates the yes person isn't the desire to be needed by others, but instead to gain the approval of others. As a child, the yes person learned that putting others first made them more likable, and came with perks, such as being the 'favorite child,' 'teacher's pet,' or savior of the day. They saw that the more useful they can be to others, the more respect they gained in the group.

Associated belief: "My value lies in what other people think about me."

7. The Idolizer/Hero-Worshiper Type

The idolizer tends to seek out people they admire, as objects to project their fantasies on. As a child, the idolizer may have internalized their feelings and felt ashamed of who they are, which caused them to see themselves as inferior to others. Alternatively, as a child, the idolizer may have been discouraged from becoming independent and was often pampered by a caretaker parent. They grow up seeking other people whom they can admire, and who would make them feel accepted and valued.

Associated belief: "I am unworthy of being loved by my hero."

You might be wondering what the seven inner girl archetypes have in common. They all stem from insecure attachments with parents and unmet emotional needs. Thus, these archetypes are patterns learned from behaviors modeled by parents, which you unconsciously keep alive in your adulthood.

Some people mistaken these archetypes as being part of their character. However, if you recall our discussion about cultural identity and how your family dynamics can affect how you see yourself, you will see how an inner girl archetype is simply a response to behaviors or experiences you witnessed from your childhood. Moreover, these inner girl archetypes are examples of the wounded inner girl, not the innocent and divine child that exists within. Therefore, your inner girl archetype cannot be likened to your personality, but rather learned behaviors stemming from a troubled childhood.

5

HEAL THE INNER GIRL

The wounded inner child is the primary gateway to healing and integration.
When you invite your woundedness out of subversiveness and into your
awareness you finally begin to honor the past pain. You also minimize its
contractive influence on your life. And you begin to offer yourself the potential of
something more.
–Markus William Kasunich

WHAT IS INNER GIRL WORK?

Inner girl work refers to the process involved in healing the wounded inner girl. This process can involve many different types of exercises and techniques, although the first step is always to connect with your inner girl.

Connecting with your inner girl simply means taking the time to focus on your inner life, including your thoughts, emotions, habits, and memories, as a way to re-experience certain life events (and the emotional experience that comes with them), so you can give yourself the closure you deserve.

Closure is something we think about when seeking to repair relationships with others. However, giving yourself closure for the experiences you had, or didn't have in the past, can set your inner girl free and give you the opportunity to redefine who you are and how you choose to live moving forward.

Be prepared to experience resistance from the addict within when you decide to start the inner girl work. Remember, the addict within? The wounded part of you that is afraid to heal and would rather "suck it up" or "grow up" than confront past suffering? It will seek to convince you not to rock the boat, or explore therapeutic exercises you have never attempted before.

But let's take a moment and think about why the addict within would be terrified of inner girl work. Picture in your mind an alcoholic named Mariah who has gotten away with being labeled as a 'social drinker' for over 10 years. Eventually, her excessive drinking starts to affect her relations with colleagues at work and close friends and family. Driven by love, Mariah's colleagues, together with a few close friends and family, stage an intervention. It is clear from their touching speeches that they are all concerned about her well-being.

However, Mariah ends up denying she has a drinking problem, and the fact that she needs help. According to her, there is nothing alarming about drinking every day, even to the detriment of her work and family life. Her colleagues and close friends and family are left speechless. They don't understand why Mariah would deny that she had a problem, or refuse getting professional help.

The addict within resists inner girl work as much as Mariah, the alcoholic, would resist rehabilitation. This isn't because there aren't any issues to fix. After all, the addict within is birthed from traumatic experiences. However, over the years, there has been so much shame and denial covering the root issues that it has caused cognitive dissonance—the phenomenon of holding two conflicting beliefs about who you are.

In other words, the addict within knows that you carry deep emotional wounds, but denies the fact that they need to be resolved, or that they are causing serious issues in your life. The same can be said about Mariah. She may admit to chugging down a case of beer every day, but denies that her drinking is interfering with other aspects of her life.

Strategies to Connect With Your inner girl

Being prepared to face resistance from the addict within is what will help you remain focused as you complete your inner girl work. As you drown out the noise from the external world and tune into the activity of your internal world, remember that recalling certain memories will bring about discomfort. Avoid going too deep into your past experiences that you re-traumatize yourself. Feeling emotional at any point during inner girl work is always a great time to pause, take a few deep breaths, and assess how you are feeling.

Here are a few ways you can begin the process of connecting to your inner girl:

- **Acknowledge that you have an inner girl.** Having an inner girl is simply acknowledging the former versions of yourself and past experiences stored in your subconscious mind. You can acknowledge your inner girl by taking the time to recall past memories and connecting to the individual you were at that time. Let her know you see her and are ready to listen to what she has to tell you.
- **Listen to your inner girl.** After you have connected with that younger self, prepare to listen to her. Put away all preconceived ideas or opinions of what your younger self may have gone through, and open your heart to feel whatever emotions start pouring out, or thoughts that suddenly flood your mind. In other words, listening to your inner girl is about freeing up space in your mind and heart so you can become an empty vessel, ready to validate your inner girl's experiences.
- **Observe your inner girl without judgment.** It is natural to find some of your inner girl's needs somewhat silly or unimportant. For instance, if you never heard your parents

tell you they loved you, then your inner girl may still be holding onto not hearing that she was loved. Remind yourself to listen and observe without judging or trivializing your inner girl's experiences. After all, most of your inner girl's issues will stem from unresolved childhood issues.

- **Write a letter to your inner girl.** Communication with your inner girl isn't a one-way process. Since you are grown up and have a more expansive view of the world, you can share insights with your inner girl and explain your childhood experiences from a new perspective. For instance, in your letter, you may be able to explain the attachment style with your parents, the impact of certain traumatic events, and other situations that you didn't understand back then. Your letter can also seek to reassure your inner girl that you are okay, and that you were able to survive those childhood experiences.

- **Speak out loud to your inner girl.** Besides writing a letter to your inner girl, you can also have verbal conversations. This helps you practice rehearsing your life story and being able to express your thoughts and emotions in words. Articulating how your thoughts and emotions bring clarity and can make you feel confident in owning your truth. In other words, the more you practice expressing how you feel, or detailing the impact of childhood experiences, the less shame or denial you will have toward your emotional wounds.

AT-HOME THERAPEUTIC EXERCISES TO HEAL YOUR INNER GIRL

Inner girl work can be done using various therapeutic exercises, and the good thing is you don't need to visit a therapist to get started. All you need to do is create a safe space for your mind and body to calm down, so you can easily tap into your subconscious mind. There are no skills you need to have beforehand to do inner girl work because your main job will be to acknowledge and observe your thoughts and emotions.

This section will introduce you to some great exercises that will help you get started with inner girl work. You may be familiar with some of these exercises, and others may be new. Give yourself the opportunity to practice each exercise at least once, and document your experience afterward. Who knows? You may just discover your new favorite form of therapy!

Lastly, as you go through each therapeutic exercise, feel free to speak to your inner girl as though you were speaking to a real person. Have meaningful conversations, ask questions, and offer plenty of reassurance and unconditional love. If you would like to give your inner girl a name, pick one that feels right to you. Naming your inner girl is a way to honor your younger self and feel more connected to a part of who you are.

Set Healthy Boundaries

For many survivors of childhood trauma, setting boundaries with others can be one of the most difficult tasks. During childhood, the lines between personal space and communal space were blurred, and many times personal boundaries were either violated or were simply not allowed.

If you lacked boundaries early in life, you may have grown up without a clear understanding of when you have overextended your-self to others, or when others have crossed your personal comfort zone. This can leave you feeling resentful for not protecting your inter-ests more effectively, or allowing others to lead your life.

Boundaries often get a bad rap. They are sometimes seen as limiting others' access to you, which can be perceived as selfish. However, there is nothing selfish about communicating your level of comfort and where your limits are.

Think about it this way: A house usually has a front door that is either open or closed. When the front door is open, guests can freely walk inside, but when it is closed, guests need to knock or come back another time. The front door of a house also protects the people inside from unwanted visitors, like thieves in the night. By locking the front door in the evenings, they are looking out for their own safety.

Boundaries are much like the front door of a house. They control the level of access others have to your life. When you set a boundary, you express your limits and what you can and cannot accept from others, and from yourself. This is done so that you can enjoy the relationships you have with others without jeopardizing your mental and emotional well-being. In essence, by enforcing healthy boundaries, you get to create the kind of relationships you never had growing up– relationships that are built on unconditional acceptance, support, and mutual respect.

Here are five types of healthy boundaries you can set with others:

1. Physical Boundaries

Physical boundaries refer to the limits you set regarding your personal space, body, and privacy. For instance, you may feel uncomfortable receiving hugs from strangers, or maybe you prefer not having friends post photos of you on social media without asking for your permission. Whatever your physical boundaries are, sharing your expectations can help you feel physically safe in the company of others. It can also help you set consequences for boundary violations. For example, you might say: "If you lay your hands on me, then I will have to break up with you."

2. Emotional Boundaries

Emotional boundaries are about drawing a line between your feelings and other people's feelings. You never have to feel responsible for another person's emotional experience, or respond to emotional needs that compromise your own emotional well-being. For example, you might create boundaries regarding what kind of sensitive information people share with you (especially if the content is triggering). You also might want to create boundaries regarding conflict resolution and how you prefer to be treated when you are upset. For example, you might tell your partner: "When I am upset, I need a few minutes to myself so I can cool down. Please don't follow after me."

3. Sexual Boundaries

Sexual boundaries refer to your preferences and limits regarding physical intimacy. Consent is extremely important when sharing your body with another person, and touch that is not warranted violates your sexual boundaries. Examples of sexual boundaries include appropriate or inappropriate forms of touch, sexual comments, and frequency of engaging in sex. If you have a history of sexual abuse, there might be certain acts that make you feel uncomfortable. It is important to communicate these with your partner to avoid being re-traumatized. For example, you might ask your partner not to touch your lower back, as this could be triggering.

4. Intellectual Boundaries

Intellectual boundaries protect your ideas, thoughts, and beliefs. Having others show respect when you are expressing your views can give you the confidence to assert your beliefs. If you feel afraid or embarrassed to share your opinions with others, an intellectual boundary may be necessary. For example, you can ask others to allow you to complete your thought before speaking, or when someone disagrees with your opinion you can ask them to refrain from hurling insults, demeaning your perspective, or making you feel inferior. For example, you might say: "It is okay to disagree with my point of view, but please don't put me down for expressing my opinion."

5. Financial Boundaries

Financial boundaries are about regulating how much access others have to your money. It is common to find partners or family members who feel entitled to their loved ones' money, and may even resort to intimidation or threats to get some money. However, how you choose to spend your money and who you choose to give it to (or invest it in), is your personal choice. It is okay to say no to money requests without explaining yourself. Moreover, you don't need to feel obliged to bail out friends and family just because you have the funds.

Your boundaries will naturally evolve over time as your needs evolve. You will need to regularly communicate your boundaries so others know how to respect your limits. Remember that saying no to others creates an immediate boundary that protects your own well-being. You don't need to feel guilty for saying no when that is genuinely how you feel because a 'no' to others is a big 'yes' to your own physical, mental, and emotional safety.

To figure out the kind of boundaries your inner girl needs in order to feel safe, simply ask the question and then close your eyes and listen for the answers. The answers may come immediately or they may take a while. Ultimately, you know deep down what kind of boundaries are lacking in your life based on the lifestyle choices or norms in your relationships that make you feel most disrespected, uncomfortable, or taken for granted.

Body Scan Meditation

A common symptom of PTSD is anxiety. When you are anxious, you may find it difficult to regulate your breathing, focus on tasks, or remain present in the moment. Anxiety activates the stress response, also known as the fight-flight-freeze response, which causes you to mentally disconnect from your body. This makes it harder to tune into your emotions and work through your emotional triggers.

The body scan meditation is a type of Vipassana meditation inspired by Eastern traditions. It seeks to bring your attention to different parts of your body through a technique known as scanning. The scan normally begins from the crown of your head and continues until you reach the tip of your toes. During the scan, your aim is to notice each body part and any tension that may be stored there, and consciously bring relief.

You can practice body scan meditation as the first step to inner girl work. It is a great way to relax your mind and body after a busy day and gently transition from thinking about the concerns of your busy lifestyle to focusing on your inner girl. The body scan meditation can also help you release negative energy from your body, such as stress or anxiety, and any form of physical tension you may have. This helps you connect deeper to your physical and emotional states, which is important when doing inner girl work.

Doing a body scan at home is fairly simple. Below is a basic guide to help you get started (feel free to personalize your meditation according to your needs):

- Get comfortable in a seated position with your back upright. Make sure that the room or area you are in is quiet and free from as many distractions as possible.
- Set a timer for 10-15 minutes.
- Gently close your eyes and bring your attention to the crown of your head. Notice any sensations you may be experiencing in that area, such as tingling, warmth, or pain. If there is any pain or tension, take a few deep breaths and imagine that with every exhale the pain or tension is leaving your body.
- Continue your scan by moving down to several different parts of your body, such as your neck, shoulders, chest area, stomach, arms, hands, and so on. As you concentrate on each body part, notice the sensations that are there and repeat the steps mentioned above to release tension.
- After scanning your toes, take a few deep breaths and scan your entire body. Notice the sensations flowing through you. You can take this opportunity to set positive intentions for your body as you prepare to do inner girl work. For example, you might think or confess: "I intend to keep my heart open as I explore a childhood memory."
- When you are ready, take three deep breaths, and gently open your eyes.

Regularly practicing this short and simple meditation can help you become more aware of bodily sensations and safely release any stress or pain in a controlled manner. Moreover, the more you learn how to sit with your discomfort, the easier you will find regulating your emotions whenever you are confronted with challenging situations.

For example, at times your inner girl may be triggered by certain people or places. Catching the trigger early enough can help you respond to your inner girl in a calm manner before reacting impulsively. Instead of shutting down when you feel offended, you might excuse yourself and take a few deep breaths, imagining that with each exhale the frustration is leaving your body. Thereafter, you can return to the conversation feeling more relaxed and prepared to have a controlled discussion.

Journaling

Many years ago, journaling was seen as a pastime hobby. Today, psychotherapists recommended journaling as a therapeutic exercise to address symptoms of PTSD. One form of journaling, expressive writing, is particularly useful in helping individuals address psychological issues and work through strong emotions like anxiety or anger. When sustained over a long period, journaling can lead to post-traumatic growth, which is the ability to see the silver lining in past traumatic experiences.

All you need to start journaling is a pen and notebook. No one else will have access to your notebook, unless you decide to share some of your entries with specific people. You can also choose to have more than one notebook so you can dedicate each one to specific themes or purposes. For example, you might have a notebook dedicated to your inner girl, another one reserved for showing gratitude, and the third notebook that deals with the theme of forgiveness.

Below are a few tips to make the most of each journaling experience:

- Dedicate a time either in the morning or in the evenings when you can journal without any interruptions. It is often recommended to journal when you are most relaxed and don't have any other urgent tasks to complete.
- Take a few minutes to reflect on how you are feeling as you are about to start journaling. Your mood can influence how you express yourself, and the perspective you write from. If you are feeling tense or distracted, take a few deep breaths or practice a body scan meditation.
- Begin writing down whatever thought that comes into your mind. If you have any journal prompts to help you, focus on answering the prompt in the most honest way possible. Remember, there are no right or wrong answers, just truthful answers that reflect your experience. Avoid proof-reading or being overly concerned with the structure of your writing or choice of words. Simply allow your pen to flow as thoughts enter your mind.
- You are not required to read what you write immediately after writing it. However, if you would like to read through your entry, you are welcome to. As you read what you wrote, maintain a non-judgmental view. If what you wrote triggers emotional distress, step away and take a moment to calm yourself. It may help to write about the same topic over and over again to gradually minimize your triggers.

If spontaneously writing down your thoughts is something you are uncomfortable with, you can use journal prompts to direct your thoughts. Here are a few journal prompts to help you connect and communicate with your inner girl:

- What is something I am judging or blaming myself for constantly?
- I want to forgive myself so I can feel…
- When I made bad choices in the past, I was motivated by [insert emotional experience].

- What is the one thing that can make me feel instantly safe?
- What are five small tasks I can do each day to show myself love?
- What am I proud of myself for?
- If I were a loving parent, what would I say to my inner girl right now?
- What is the positive affirmation or mantra I can live by this week?

Art Therapy

The inner girl is naturally creative, although this creativity may have been stifled or ridiculed during childhood. Nonetheless, expressive art is still a great way to connect with the inner girl and convey deep emotions you may feel uncomfortable writing about.

Inner girl drawings, is a type of art therapy, which helps you tap into your subconscious mind. The drawings are typically done with your least utilized hand (if you are right-handed, then you would draw with your left hand), to prevent you from controlling the process. Ultimately, it is your inner girl that leads, and your job is to support your inner girl's creative process.

Challenge yourself to complete an inner girl drawing for 30 days. On each day, draw a picture on a clean page using all sorts of fun and different coloring pencils and tools. If you would like, you can make a note about what you felt during and after each drawing.

Follow these instructions for carrying out your 30-day inner girl drawing challenge:

- Set aside time alone with your sketchbook and some coloring pencils.
- Close your eyes and take a moment to connect to your inner girl. It may help to create a mental picture of who she is, how she looks, and what she is feeling in that particular moment.

- Invite your inner girl to take the lead as you draw a picture together. Each day, you can decide on what kind of image you are going to draw. For instance, it could be an image of your inner girl, an image of a past memory as your inner girl recalls it, or an image of a deep emotion your inner girl is feeling.
- Give your inner girl as much time as they need to draw the picture. Encourage your inner girl to be as expressive as they are comfortable being.
- After the drawing is complete, thank your inner girl for expressing her thoughts and emotions on the page. Thereafter, observe the drawing to gain understanding of your inner girl's perspective.

Practice Self-Care

Practicing self-care isn't exactly a therapeutic exercise, although it can enhance your quality of life and help you respond to the needs of your inner girl. When most people think about self-care, they think of running a hot bubble bath and burning a fragrant candle. And while this can be a form of self-care, it isn't necessarily all that self-care is cut out to be.

Self-care isn't merely about tantalizing your taste buds or pampering yourself at a day spa. Instead, the crux of self-care is responding to your physical, mental, emotional, and spiritual needs. So, think about it for a moment: Do you *need* a bubble bath, or do you *need* some time to rest and relax? The truth is your need for rest and relaxation is what causes you to run bath water and soak in the tub for countless hours. Therefore, self-care is about being aware of your human needs, throughout the day, and finding ways to respond to those needs by practicing various activities.

If responding to your needs was that simple, perhaps we wouldn't have a whole section in the book dedicated to self-care. Oftentimes, practicing self-care can make you feel guilty, as though responding to your human needs is a luxury, or something you haven't yet earned.

How many times have you heard people say: "I'll sleep after I have completed these tasks," or "I can't afford to take a break?" Even though their survival depends on how well they take care of themselves, most people don't prioritize—or feel ashamed of prioritizing—self-care.

There is nothing indulgent or selfish about identifying personal needs and responding to them. In fact, neglecting your needs can put a strain on your relationships, since you heavily rely on those around you to fulfill those needs. And in other instances, neglecting your needs can lead to burn out, mental illness, and other psychological issues.

However, let's backtrack and try to trace where your self-neglect or self-denial may come from. Think back to your childhood, or at least 15 to 20 years ago. Recall a time when you were made to feel bad for putting your needs first. Perhaps you were raised by a parent who wanted all the attention in the house focused on them. Or maybe you grew up in a highly moral or religious family where it was seen as taboo to consider your own needs.

During that time, what kinds of beliefs did your inner girl create about self-care? Did they believe that self-care was wrong? Or immoral? And how did you perceive people who practiced self-care? Were they wasteful? Or self-absorbed? Your level of comfortability in practicing self-care is linked to how self-care was introduced (if at all) during your childhood. If thinking about your needs was unacceptable, then even in your adult years, you might view your needs as being trivial.

Since responding to your needs is crucial to your survival, you open yourself up to mental, emotional, and physical illness when you don't make a point to fulfill your needs. Moreover, the longer you neglect your needs and focus on responding to others' needs instead, the more it becomes a habit. In other words, you start to derive pleasure (remember the dopamine rush?) from taking care of others, rather than feeling immense satisfaction in taking care of yourself first.

Reclaiming your sense of self-worth begins with making self-care a priority. If it has never been a priority in your life before, now you have the opportunity to know what it feels like to achieve wholeness through healthy and positive practices, rather than maladaptive coping strategies that may lead to all sorts of addiction. In essence, the same dopamine rush that you may get from taking care of others can be experienced when you start treating your mind, body, and soul with compassion.

To ensure that you are responding to various types of needs, you can break down self-care into three different components: physical, mental, and emotional. Below are suggestions of different activities you can incorporate into your lifestyle to respond to your physical, mental, and emotional self-care.

1. Physical Self-Care

Your basic physical needs include things like food, proper shelter, and clothing. However, once your basic needs have been addressed, you can improve your overall health by watching what you eat, incorporating physical exercise into your lifestyle, or spending time outdoors and getting much needed sunlight. Here are a few activities you can practice to improve your physical self-care:

- Close your eyes and take a few deep and meaningful breaths.
- Take a short nap.
- Prepare your favorite meal from scratch.
- Take your prescribed medication.
- Boost your water intake.
- Declutter your house.
- Stretch your body or go on a brisk walk.
- Change your bed sheets and linen.

2. Mental Self-Care

Mental self-care involves responding to mental needs, such as the need for mental clarity, relaxation, and lowered stress. The great thing about practicing mental self-care is that it won't take much of your time. In between daily tasks, or when you get some free time, you can take mental health check-ins and practice the following activities:

- Read a chapter of a book.
- Complete a short guided meditation.
- Create a list of tasks you need to complete for the day.
- Close your eyes and visualize the healed inner girl.
- Call a close friend or family member.
- Write down the pros and cons of a decision you plan to make.
- Clear your email mailbox.
- Delete apps that consume a lot of time.
- Listen to soothing or uplifting music.

3. Emotional Self-Care

Emotional self-care involves responding to emotional needs, such as acknowledging your feelings, setting boundaries with others, practicing gratitude, or catching up with a close friend. Below are some of the activities you can practice to improve your emotional self-care:

- Schedule an appointment with a therapist.
- Write in your journal.
- Recite positive affirmations.
- Write a letter to your inner girl.
- Send a text to a close friend or family member.
- Watch a show that makes you laugh.
- Listen to a motivational podcast.
- Spend time cuddling with your pet—or significant other.
- Mute or block social media accounts that are negative or lower your self-esteem.
- Set new short and long-term goals.
- Volunteer at a local charity.

On top of practicing physical, mental, and emotional self-care, it is important to create a healthy living space and work environment. For example, if you are working at a company that brings a lot of stress and compromises your mental health, consider changing work teams or departments, or start looking for a job that is aligned to your interests and supports the kind of lifestyle you are seeking.

Or if you are living in a household where there is constant conflict, or poor eating choices are made, consider introducing rules for conflict resolution, or promoting cooking food from scratch instead of buying takeout. These small lifestyle changes are alternative forms of self-care that can improve the quality of your life.

Now that you have the tools to begin healing the wounded inner girl, we can move on to a crucial aspect of healing psychological trauma, which is healing the addict within. How can you heal this broken part of yourself? By confronting your shadow and committing to shadow work.

6

HEAL THE ADDICT WITHIN THROUGH SHADOW WORK

We're afraid that if we fully surrender to our darkness, we'll never come back from it. We're afraid our darkness will go on and on and on, that there is no end to it and that we will get lost in it. We're afraid that if we show these ugly, unpalatable parts of ourselves, it will be too much for others; that nobody will love and accept us, and we'll be left alone with only the worst parts of ourselves for company.
–Evanna Lynch

WHAT IS THE SHADOW?

You have been introduced to several terms throughout this book, such as the 'addict within,' inner girl, and now, the shadow. All of these terms describe non-physical aspects of who you are, which directly or indirectly affect your psyche.

We have said that the addict within is that part of you that developed as a result of past challenges and traumatic events. Although it recognizes the need for healing, the addict within is riddled with shame and denial. It seeks by all means to hide, numb, or escape the pain of yesteryears by turning to maladaptive behaviors or chemical and behavioral addictions.

Furthermore, we described the inner girl as the personification of your subconscious mind. Your inner girl is neither good nor bad, but simply serves as a mirror to the beliefs and emotions you have stored deep in your mind. If you suffered abuse or neglect as a child and were not able to get closure, your inner girl will act out this trauma through unhealthy habits, self-limiting beliefs, and behaviors.

So, what is the shadow? And how does it relate to the addict within and the inner girl? The shadow refers to the dark aspects of your personality that form part of the bigger picture of who you are. If you were to take a bird's eye view of your personality, you would see that you are not one dimensional. You can be generous and self-serving, confident and insecure, accepting of others and judgmental.

Since childhood, you were taught to hide or reject these dark aspects of your personality because they were seen as character defects or flaws. Perhaps you came from a family that emphasized upholding moral virtues and traits like selfishness, jealousy, or the lack of self-control were seen as weaknesses. Thus, instead of owning your dark qualities and learning how to integrate them into the broader picture of who you are, you pushed them deep down into your psyche—so far down that they were difficult to trace.

The concept of shadow was another one of Jung's discoveries. He challenged how well people really know themselves, and which aspects of themselves they claimed to love. According to Jung, people distance themselves from behaviors, characteristics, thoughts, and emotions they consider dangerous. Danger in this sense could refer to external consequences (i.e., Losing the favor of others and being isolated from the community) and internal consequences (i.e., Having an identity crisis and being overwhelmed with grief).

Pretending the shadow doesn't exist is part of the role and responsibility of the addict within because if you deny the aspects of yourself that terrorize you, then you won't need to face them. Of course, as we have seen with many people who deny trauma, these dark traits manifest in other ways, such as aggression, impulsive behavior, mood swings, anxiety, and perverted thoughts. Therefore, as much as you can pretend to not have a shadow, you cannot contain the urges, impulses, and obsessions that result from overlooking this aspect of who you are.

Denying your shadow can lead to you developing shadow behaviors. Here are a few examples of what shadow behaviors look like:

- **Being quick to judge others who have a different worldview than you.** You see yourself as knowing more than others and seek to correct or condemn behaviors that are not aligned to how you view the world.
- **Projecting your insecurities onto others.** You may feel upset when you see others displaying qualities that you are too afraid to display within yourself. For example, you might label an outspoken person as arrogant, not because they are conceited, but because you resent their ability to speak their mind so freely.
- **Having a short-temper with people you deem lower than you in position or class.** You tend to assert dominance over people who you see as inferior as a way to compensate for your own feelings of inferiority or helplessness.
- **Playing the role of the victim when you don't want to accept responsibility.** Instead of admitting that you were wrong, you find ways of turning the tables and gaining sympathy from others. Playing the victim keeps you from confronting aspects of your personality that are harmful to yourself and others.
- **The willingness to deceive others if it means getting ahead in life.** You place your survival at the center of your life, even if it means having to compromise your relationships with others.
- **Feeling like there is nothing you can do wrong.** You have what is known as a "messiah complex" that makes you believe there is nothing you can do wrong, and instead it is your job to save people and help them get rid of their shadows.

Having to confront some of these behaviors in yourself is extremely difficult, and this is the reason why the shadow remains a hidden part of your subconscious. It is as though your mind cannot accept the possibility of having both good and dark qualities; however, it doesn't have a problem with identifying good and dark qualities in others.

In fact, identifying some of these shadow behaviors in others makes the mind feel good. It affirms that there are others who are more troubled, cruel, or dangerous than you, and therefore, you are not as "psychologically sick" as the next person. Jung observed this phenomenon in people and came to the conclusion that we often reject our own flaws and project them onto others. In other words, we have a tendency to see in others what we cannot accept, express, or heal within ourselves.

For example, take Sam who is in a new romantic relationship with Jerry. Due to Sam's troubled relationship with her parents, which ultimately led to her being homeless at 18, she has difficulty trusting men. However, Sam is not ready to accept the pain she has been carrying since childhood and how it negatively impacts her relationship. Instead of admitting she has trust issues, she often accuses Jerry of infidelity or makes him feel guilty for establishing boundaries.

Sam believes that the conflict in her relationship would end if Jerry would simply be more transparent. But the truth is no matter how transparent Jerry can be, it won't take away Sam's trust issues. Essentially, the best way to resolve conflict in their relationship would be for Sam to confront her shadow and work through her feelings of distrust.

How to Perform Shadow Work?

Jung once said, "Until you make the unconscious conscious, it will direct your life and you will call it fate" (Othon, 2017). For Jung, the best way to acknowledge and embrace the shadow was to perform shadow work. Shadow work involves uncovering the thoughts, emotions, and desires that have been repressed for many years and bringing them to light.

Instead of thinking that you know yourself, you take a step back and journey into your subconscious with the intention to learn more about yourself. Shadow work is in no way an act of condemnation or feeling guilty for identifying hidden impulses or motivations. The only goal is to gain a deeper awareness of your good and dark qualities, without assigning labels or making any judgments.

As you gain more awareness about who you are, how you think, and the hidden intentions behind your actions, you can ask your inner girl questions to gain insight. For example, upon discovering that the reason behind your 'silent treatment' during conflict is to gain an upper hand in the argument, you might pause and ask: *"Why do I react this way?"* This simple question might take you on a whole different journey into a past memory where giving someone the silent treatment made them give into your demands. In other words, by observing the shadow and asking your inner girl questions, you can trace your dark traits to core memories or core emotional wounds.

As you observe your shadow, you may be confronted with another question: *"Am I really a bad person?"*

Before you start overthinking and entering a spiral of negative thoughts, consider which aspect of you might be asking this question. Which 'self' would care to ask if they are a bad person or not? Is it the five-year-old girl who was told that she was wrong for refusing to be hugged? The 16-year-old young lady who was rejected by her friends after choosing to date the high school jock? Or the 28-year-old woman who finally ended an abusive relationship with her longtime partner?

Once you have identified you are asking the question, you can respond in a compassionate way, being as truthful and reassuring as you can. For example, you might tell the five-year-old girl: *"Your physical safety is more important than others' need to embrace you. You were not wrong for refusing to be hugged because you didn't feel comfortable being embraced by that individual. I am sorry that you have carried this feeling of guilt for all these years. I am here to relieve you of this guilt."*

The same process can be followed when you find yourself feeling

ANNE LUNAR

ashamed for identifying emotions like jealousy, resentment, or cyni-
cism in yourself. Take a moment to pause and consider which 'self'
feels ashamed for feeling jealous, resentful, or cynical. Go back into
the past and trace situations that made you feel these emotions.

Show compassion to that younger self that felt jealous, resentful,
or cynical. Step into their shoes and empathize with what they must
have been going through at the time. Thereafter, tell your younger self
that there is no need to feel ashamed for having these emotions. They
are natural reactions to situations we deem threatening. Therefore,
your younger self isn't a bad person for having these emotions.

SHADOW WORK AND THE I-GIRL PROCESS

Shadow work can help you cultivate a deeper appreciation for who you
are. However, even more than that, it can positively change how you
interact with the world. Through shadow work, you can see that the
world is as broken or as healed as your own heart. You become more
aware of what you hate or fear, so that you no longer have to project
your hatred or fear onto others.

The statement "hurt people hurt people," is painfully true.
Although another statement also rings true: Hurt people hurt
themselves.

By doing shadow work, you can finally slay the demons that have
been governing your behaviors and causing you to wreak havoc in
your life and in the lives of those around you. The deeper your awareness of your shadow grows, the more conscious you will become
about what you say, how you behave, and the impact of your decisions
on others.

The I-GIRL process is a useful guide to help you connect with your
inner girl and work through your shadow behaviors. The acronym
stands for:

- I = Invite and Connect
- G = Go Deeper
- I = Initiate Action

72

- R = Recognize and Resolve
- L = Letting In and Letting Go

The I-GIRL process begins with you. Are you ready to stop reacting unconsciously and take responsibility for your actions and inactions? Are you prepared to turn inward and question yourself, rather than pointing fingers? If so, the following five steps will help you identify, accept, love, embody, and integrate your shadow in every area of your life.

Step 1: Invite and Connect

Before you can begin shadow work, you need to prepare your environment for the work. This means going into a quiet room where you can spend 15-30 uninterrupted minutes by yourself. You will also need a few materials, such as a pen, notebook, coloring pencils (if you desire to draw), a cozy blanket, and some warm tea or snacks. The more comfortable you are, the smoother the process will flow.

Next, you will need to invite your inner girl into the room. In other words, you will need to relax your mind and body and prepare to tap into your thoughts and emotions. A body scan meditation or creating a mental picture of your inner girl can help you create a connection.

When you are ready to begin the shadow work, you can ask your inner girl general questions like how she is doing, or what's on her mind. At this point, you might get an image or memory of a past experience in your mind. Without drawing any conclusions in your mind, observe the image or memory and ask yourself the following questions:

- What has happened?
- Why do you feel the way that you do?
- Who was involved in the situation?
- When did this situation happen?
- Where did the situation take place?

- How can you help your inner girl heal and move forward from this?

Step 2: Go Deeper

This step leads on from the previous one. Based on what your inner girl desires to share with you at that moment, your job will be to probe deeper so you can understand her perspective. You can do this by writing down answers to 'why' questions in your journal. For example, if your inner girl brings up a memory of feeling resentment toward your parents, the first question you would pose to your inner girl is: *"What am I feeling?"* followed by a series of 'why' questions. Here is an example:

What am I feeling: Resentment toward my parents.
Why: I felt neglected as a child because they were focused on building their careers rather than raising me.
Why: Work was more of a priority than parenting.
Why: Work made them feel successful, but coming from broken homes, they never saw what healthy parenting looked like.

You will notice that 'why' questions take you into a rabbit-hole of thought. Where you eventually end up looks very different from where you began. For example, your inner girl brings up resentment toward your parents. As you probe, you discover that your resentment comes from feeling neglected as a child. However, you also start to see that the same neglect you felt, your parents felt as a result of how they were raised. In other words, you realize that your parents could not give you something they were not given (or witnessed) as children either.

Step 3: Initiate Action

At this stage, you understand your inner girl's perspective better and may even have gained insight about what was actually happening or why it happened the way it did. You can see what needs to be addressed, but before jumping into making changes, create a solid plan on how to do this.

Using the example from above, your goal would be to address your feelings of resentment toward your parents. There are many different ways you can go about doing that, such as seeing a therapist, writing a letter to your parents, or practicing radical acceptance of the situation. You can also work on accepting your resentment by practicing meditation and allowing yourself to feel the emotion move through and out of your body. You may still feel resentful afterward, but the more you become familiar with the emotion, the less triggering it will become.

Step 4: Recognize and Resolve

Reaching the fourth step requires a lot of work. So far, you have taken the time to listen to your inner girl, identified emotional wounds or shadow behaviors that need to be addressed, and created a plan of action. With this plan, you will start to resolve your issues, but remember that healing emotional wounds or learning to embrace dark traits takes time. Be sure to carve out time each day to practice a therapeutic exercise like journaling or drawing, and don't be afraid to reach out to your support network.

Step 5: Letting In and Letting Go

Acknowledging past hurt and embracing undesirable qualities about yourself can feel like walking across an auditorium full of people, naked. As you accept that you are not the saint you thought you were, nor are you the monster that others paint you out to be, you become more vulnerable and open to expressing every aspect of who you are.

Allowing yourself to be unashamedly you is an act of courage. You give yourself the permission to let go of the survival mindset of "being accepted by others" and embrace the complexity of who you are. Others who look upon you may judge you for openly embracing traits they deem unacceptable, but remember that is merely projection. You no longer have any reason to hide aspects of yourself that you have come to unconditionally love!

Once these five steps have been followed, you will experience a stronger mind and heart coherence, and will feel more connected with your inner girl. The only thing left is to remember to bring your shadow along with you as you journey through life, so you don't unintentionally empower the addict within.

PART IV

FROM ADDICT TO ADVOCATE

7

RETURN TO COMMUNITY

*Only through the group, I realized—through sharing the suffering of the group—
could the body reach that height of existence that the individual alone could
never attain. And for the body to reach that level at which the divine might be
glimpsed, a dissolution of individuality was necessary.*
–Yukio Mishima

THE JOURNEY FROM ADDICT TO ADVOCATE

Charles Bukowski once said, "You have to die a few times before you
can really live" (Leobart, 2020). If you look back at your life and all
the experiences you have overcome, you may identify several
moments where it felt like your world was collapsing. Perhaps it was
the death of a loved one, a painful breakup, or having your creature
comforts taken away.

According to Bukowski, these 'deaths' are the catalyst for positive
change; the opportunity to redefine who you are and live a meaningful
life. But the ability to withstand so many devastating life experiences
is not easy. It takes several years to gather yourself from events that
shook your entire existence, and even so, there is no guarantee of
healing on the other side.

However, our message is one of hope. Without hoping that recovery from addiction is possible, and that one day your inner girl will be free from pain, then there is no motivation to reevaluate your life. You have experienced many dark days and even came close to giving up on yourself, but hope is what kept you fighting.

In fact, hope is what has carried you throughout this book until this point. It is obvious that you desire healing, and by focusing on this desire, you are able to open your mind and heart to the possibility of healing. You have been so brave to reflect on your own life and ask yourself difficult questions about your actions and behaviors. The positive intention to heal that you have released into the atmosphere will create a ripple effect of positive change.

In this final portion of the book, we will look at intentional life-style choices you can make to facilitate your healing journey. In particular, we will focus on lost traditions that are overlooked in modern society, such as the value of community, finding your purpose, connecting to spirituality, and opening your heart to love.

It is possible for you to switch from an addict to an advocate and regain control of your life. All it takes is making conscious choices to lead with love and pay careful attention to the inner girl within.

THE RISK OF INDIVIDUALISM

Individualistic cultures promote the needs of the individual over the needs of the community. Phrases like, "It's a dog-eat-dog world," or "You've got to look out for yourself," describe the 'me versus others' mentality of individualistic cultures. Even social attitudes tend to be informed by individual preferences. For example, being self-sufficient and not relying on others for social or economic support is seen as a strength in these cultures.

Most Western societies promote individualism, although individualism can also be valued in certain workplaces, families, or social circles. There are a few striking characteristics of an individualistic culture, such as:

- Depending on others is seen as a sign of weakness or an embarrassment.
- Being independent is highly praised.
- The rights of individuals are upheld higher than the rights of the group.
- Individuals are encouraged to stand out and showcase their differences.
- A greater emphasis is placed on individualistic goals like climbing the career ladder, than collective goals like starting a family.

While independence is good, it can at times deter people from leaning on each other, especially during difficult times. For instance, in collectivist cultures, people see themselves as being part of a community and are likely to turn to their friends and family for support. Those that live in individualistic cultures have no real sense of what community means and might isolate themselves from others whenever they are facing crises (since depending on others would be shameful).

Individualistic cultures are also known to praise people who solve problems on their own and achieve goals with little to zero assistance from others. These champions are called "self-made millionaires" or "supermoms" and their extraordinary self-effort places an expectation on others to pull themselves up and wrestle through life alone.

Research has shown that social support, especially during acute or chronic stress, can positively impact an individual's mental health. Psychiatrist, Dr. Patrick Bracken, has argued that traditionally, social support used to protect communities from the impact of traumatic events (Whitley, 2017). For instance, returning soldiers who were presumably suffering from PTSD were given emotional support by their friends and family and treated like heroes. Moreover, on a governmental level, programs like the U.S. GI Bill and the Veterans Administration offered returning soldiers special benefits and services for them and their families.

The rise in individualism has also coincided with a rise in depression rates and suicide. One study showed that out of 364 districts of England, the areas with the highest increases in rates of young male suicide also had the largest population of people living alone and lowest population of married couples (Crawford & Prince, 1999).

For this reason, the role of community continues to be important as part of the process of healing trauma. It is no coincidence that social institutions like Alcoholics Anonymous host weekly meetings as part of the addict's rehabilitation. This initiative could be seen as a way to help the addict rebuild social networks they may be lacking, and learn to depend on others for emotional support.

What Is the Meaning of Community?

Have you ever thought about what community means to you? Close your eyes and picture for a moment that you are part of a community. Who are you with? Where are you? What are you doing? And what are the kinds of conversations you are having?

It is difficult to define community because it means something different to everybody. If you ask one person to define a community, they might mention their close friends and family. However, another person might mention their online gaming community or sports club. For this reason, we can loosely define community as an organized network of individuals with common goals or interests, who share and collaborate on ideas, knowledge, and resources. From this definition, there are a few components that define any community:

- **There is something you share in common.** You don't need to be blood-relatives with someone to cultivate a strong bond. What often connects you to others is sharing something in common, such as being part of the same religion, working in the same company, or being on a similar self-improvement journey.
- **You care about each other.** Not only do you have something in common with another person, but you care about their progress, well-being, and take interest in their

life. This care may be shown by asking questions, making time to see each other, and offering support.

- **You are willing to share and collaborate.** What makes communities strong is the wealth of skills and knowledge that are shared among members. Since no one knows everything, communities depend on the experiences of each individual to help the collective survive. Thus, you are able to seek help from others when you need something, and are open to helping others when they request help from you.

There is a difference between being part of a community and feeling a sense of community. For example, by social arrangement, you are already part of several communities. You already have a family, you live in a certain neighborhood, and you work at a certain company. Those are three communities you already have membership to. However, this doesn't mean that you necessarily feel safe and cared for by these communities.

The truth is we can't make people love and accept us, no matter how close we may be to them or how much we desire to be close to them. And unfortunately, as much as we can be connected with many people, not everybody will make us feel like we belong. Feeling a sense of community is that freedom you get when you are comfortable being yourself around others; when you don't need to perform or hide certain aspects of yourself. Not every relationship, workplace, or social group will provide you with that sense of community, but this is okay. All it means is that you need more time to find "your people."

When looking for your people, remember the following tips:

- **Don't be afraid to mingle with different people.** Get to know people from different cultural, education, and social backgrounds. This might encourage you to express who you are more easily since you are not restrained by your own cultural or social norms.
- **Embrace the discomfort of opening up to others.** It isn't easy to get to know new people because it requires you to

be vulnerable. However, take this as a positive thing! Your ability to be vulnerable is what helps you walk in your truth with greater conviction.

- **Accept that the best relationships take time.** Get to know people at your own pace and without any expectations. Simply enjoy every honest interaction you have with others and allow your relationships to progress naturally.

- **Look for multiple people to respond to multiple needs.** It is unfair to rely on one or two individuals to provide you with various types of support. Lighten the load on your loved ones by seeking different people to take care of different needs. For example, you can turn to a therapist if you need emotional support, seek out a mentor if you are looking for career support, or join a wellness community if you are looking for people who share the same lifestyle as you.

- **Follow your gut instinct when getting to know people.** Notice how you feel when engaging with certain people. Do you feel settled? As though you were in the company of an old friend? Or are you guarded and carefully filtering what you say? Your gut instinct will never fail you when choosing the right people to be around. Essentially, "your people" will make you feel good about being you, rather than making you feel the need to hide parts of you.

COURAGE TO ASK FOR HELP

Asking for help is generally stigmatized in highly individualistic cultures. There is an unspoken expectation for individuals to carry themselves, even when they have a solid support network within reach. Part of this is due to the emphasis on independence, but another part is due to the fear of what others might think when asking for help.

Let's face it—asking for help is seen as a form of neediness, and neediness can be seen as a sign of immaturity or lack of responsibility for one's own life. But what if asking for help isn't the same as being needy? What if instead it is a sign of courage?

Being needy and having needs are two different things. When you are needy, you rely on others to take responsibility for your well-being. You might constantly seek reassurance from a friend to compensate for your feelings of inadequacy, or depend on others' financial contributions to maintain your lifestyle.

On the other hand, having needs is a survival response. Every human being has needs, ranging from basic needs like food and shelter to psychological needs like a sense of belonging. It is a tall ask to expect any individual to respond to all of these needs by themselves, which explains why we seek jobs, friendships, hobbies, counseling, or a sense of community.

Asking for help is admitting that you need assistance in responding to your needs. It isn't the same as sitting back and depending on others to take care of you. This is why asking for help requires so much courage. First, you must risk being seen as needy, particularly, if you live in an individualistic society. And second, you must admit your own limitations and look for people who can help you overcome certain challenges.

Perhaps your inner girl needs to hear that she was brave for asking for help, even though she faced rejection or was told that it was wrong. Take a moment right now and let her know how proud you are that she was able to seek help. Reassure her that you are available whenever she needs anything from you. There is no ask that is too big for you to recognize and resolve.

Next, close your eyes and bring up a picture of the word 'no.' Slowly zoom into the picture, making it brighter, bolder, and bigger. As you come closer to the picture, check-in on your body and connect with what you are feeling. Do you feel your throat constricting? Heartbeat racing? Now, think back to a time in the past when you felt anxious after hearing the word 'no.' What went through your mind at that moment? And what story or belief did you create? Did you tell yourself that asking for help is risky? Or that no one really cares about your needs? Sit with this memory for a while so you can understand your inner girl's reluctance to ask for help.

Finally, take out your pen and notebook and write your inner girl a letter, validating her experience and giving your perspective on the word 'no.' From your fresh eyes and open heart, explain to your inner girl the benefits of hearing no, like how hearing no can simply be a redirection to a better solution, or how hearing no can help you refine your goals. Write each benefit in a convincing way, as though you were pitching to a board of directors. This will help you challenge the stigma you might have about asking for help.

You exist part of an ecosystem of people. You are never alone, even though you might isolate yourself at times. Asking for help is part of the luxury of being part of an ecosystem of people. Different forms of help are available everywhere you turn! You are courageous when you admit that you need help because you are choosing to put yourself out there and risk hearing no. But how bad is hearing no after all? Not as bad as pretending to be coping when in fact you need medical assistance, encouragement, or nurturing.

8

RETURN TO PURPOSE

Once you start recognizing the truth of your story, finish the story. It happened but you're still here, you're still capable, powerful, you're not your circumstance. It happened and you made it through. You're still fully equipped with every single tool you need to fulfill your purpose.
–Steve Maraboli

LIVE A LIFE OF PURPOSE

Every now and again, you might find yourself in a rut. Your life is neither moving backward nor moving forward, and as comfortable as it is to live this way, it doesn't bring fulfillment. The longer you stay in a rut, the more frustrated you become with your life. You see others living what seems to be a meaningful life and wonder: *"What is the meaning of my life?"*

Deep down, what you yearn for is a direction in life. Having a sense of direction is what would ground you and bring much needed consistency and stability to your life. Furthermore, having a sense of direction would help you stay away from harmful habits that would lead you into the arms of obsessions and addictions.

Finding your life's purpose, or living a life of purpose, is what can provide you with a sense of direction. It can strategically narrow your life so that you are spending most of your time and energy on tasks, passions, and goals that bring you the most satisfaction.

It is difficult to define what purpose is because it means something different to each individual. But in general terms, we can define purpose as the reason behind your existence. Purpose explains why you were born and guides you on how to live your life to ensure you make the greatest impact. Purpose is also what keeps you going and protects you from getting stuck in a rut. When you know that you are here on earth on an assignment, you have the courage to pick yourself up after a setback and redirect your life on a better path.

It's important to note that living a life of purpose is more than setting and achieving goals. Of course, pursuing goals is necessary when walking on purpose, but you should see it as a tactic, rather than the objective. It is still possible to live a purposeful life without striving toward goals—simply opening your heart to the experience of life is a noble purpose–and one that many spiritual leaders possess.

Additionally, a purposeful life is more than the work you do. Yes, we know of many people who have found purpose in their careers, but this doesn't apply to everybody. When you think of your life's purpose, you should seek to silence your mind so that you can connect with your heart's desires. Your heart, rather than your mind, is where you connect with the divine and understand the meaning of your existence. Now, if that meaning is to become a doctor and save lives, that is wonderful. However, that meaning won't always be related to your occupation.

Please do not rush the process of connecting to your life's purpose. This will only cause you to think more than you allow yourself to feel. It is only through feeling that you can receive that "Aha" moment and feel a sense of conviction about how you are destined to live your life.

It is also important to challenge any limiting beliefs you might have about connecting to your purpose. For example, if you were told as a child that you will never amount to anything, or that similar to your relatives you were destined to enter a certain career, you will need to challenge those beliefs. Remember, purpose cannot be found outside of who you are. Your purpose is part of your DNA and something that no one else can predict or control. Below are a few affirmations you can recite in front of a mirror to prepare your heart for the journey of connecting to your purpose:

- I welcome the spontaneous ideas, memories, and feelings that will come to me as I seek to discover my purpose.
- Deep down, I know what my life purpose is. I only need to remember it.
- I believe that it is possible to live out my purpose.
- I welcome the positive changes that will come as a result of living out my purpose.
- I can trust myself to know when I have remembered my purpose.

Four Activities to Inspire Purpose

You can find your purpose spontaneously as you are loading the dishwasher or having a meaningful conversation with a friend. Or you can find your purpose by engaging in specific activities. What is important when seeking your purpose is to surround yourself with people, places, and things that are inspiring and either get you to use your imagination or pull at your heartstrings. In essence, you want to remain open-hearted and sensitive to signs and synchronicities all around you. Below are four activities that can inspire purpose:

1. Reading

Reading is an activity that encourages you to tap into your imagination. Depending on what you are reading, you can learn more about who you are and begin to look at your life differently. For example, after reading this book, I assure you that you won't walk away the same. This is due to the amount of introspection that has been promoted throughout each chapter. Get into the habit of reading books that spark curiosity, challenge social conventions, and give you the opportunity to connect with hidden parts of yourself.

2. Share Your Experiences

If you are someone who believes that everything happens for a reason, then you will understand that even suffering has a purpose. In other words, your life experiences (the good and bad) are what inspire you to desire change, both in your life and in the lives of others. Sharing your experiences is about helping others get through similar life situations that you have overcome. The way in which you choose to share your experiences may be connected to your life's purpose.

3. Practice Gratitude

Gratitude is an attitude that you have everything you need, right now, to live a fulfilling life. When you are grateful for your life, you are satisfied with who you are, where you are, and what you have. Studies have shown that being content with your life can make you feel deeply connected to something greater than yourself. It causes you to realize the magnitude of the universe and how much abundance is all around you. Every task you do feels significant because you recognize that it has a far-reaching impact. Living your life in this manner will help you connect to a dream that is bigger than you and can add meaning to your life.

4. Tell Your Story

Journaling and speaking to others can also inspire your purpose. When you are expressing your thoughts and emotions through verbal or written speech, it is the same as reinforcing what you know, feel, and believe. For example, have you ever had an "Aha" moment while sharing a story with someone? As you spoke, you were able to remember certain details or challenge your own ideas? Or better yet, have you ever shared a story, and based on the amazement of the listener, you realized that what you had said was deeply profound? Whether it is through writing or talking, re-telling your stories can provide clarity about your life and help you make sense of your experiences.

FIND PURPOSE BY CONNECTING TO YOUR INNER GIRL

If finding your purpose is about connecting to your heart, then perhaps your purpose is connected to things you have always been drawn to since you were a child. Back then, when you imagined your future, you envisioned living a life that would be richly satisfying— even if what you imagined wasn't practical. You didn't worry about how your dream life would unfold or what it would take from you to make it happen. All you cared about was the fantasy and hoping one day it would manifest.

What happened to your childhood aspirations? How did they disappear? Was it due to being forced to grow up before your time? Did you have cynical parents who mocked you for daydreaming? Take a moment right now and ask your inner girl what happened to your childhood aspirations.

There were childhood ideas and desires that were typical of being a child, growing up in a certain environment. But then there were also some childhood ideas and desires that were actually connected to your purpose. Even though these ideas and desires are deep in your subconscious mind, they can be rediscovered. "How?" You may ask. The following steps will help you pull up childhood desires linked to your purpose. Note, you will need to invite your inner girl into the room and allow her to lead the rediscovery (trust me, she knows the map of your inner life more than you do).

Step 1: Reflect on Your Motivations

Working together with your inner girl, write down your motivations in life. Consider things that carry the most significance to you. They can be extrinsic motivations (gaining some sort of external reward or achievement) or intrinsic motivations (feeling a sense of inner satisfaction). What you write down may surprise you, but that doesn't mean it's wrong.

Step 2: Look for Childhood Themes

Take a trip down memory lane and think of activities you were preoccupied with as a child. These could be activities that you spent a lot of time on (voluntarily) or activities you thought about often. In your journal, write down your experience performing these activities. Be sure to mention the processes you would undertake and how these activities made you feel.

Step 3: Compare Your Motivations to Childhood Themes

Look at both your list of motivations in life and the journal entries about the activities you enjoyed as a child. Are there any similarities? What motivations can you trace back to those early childhood activities? Making the comparison should show you that the things you deeply care about today are things you cared about when you were still a kid, and probably couldn't make sense of why you enjoyed certain activities.

It is no coincidence that you have always gravitated to specific people, subjects, or passions. Your heart has always attempted to steer you in a particular direction that leads to your life's purpose. Now that you are aware that some of your ideas and desires are not random, you have the opportunity to conduct further research and ensure they come to life!

HOW TO MAKE EACH DAY MEANINGFUL

Even though it is a worthy pursuit to find your purpose, we know that it takes time. For instance, there is still a lot of inner child work and shadow work you will need to do before you can fully connect to your heart. However, just because finding your life's purpose takes time, doesn't mean you can't make each day feel meaningful.

Since meaning can be defined in many ways and assigned to different things, what constitutes a meaningful day for you might not be the same for someone else. Therefore, to gain more value out of each day, you will need to sit down and think about the kind of tasks, routines, goals, and behaviors that would put your inner girl at ease and make you feel good about your life. Here are a few pointers to help you:

1. Listen to Your Gut

Your intuition is the inner knowing that guides and protects you. It seeks to help you walk in your truth and make decisions that are beneficial for what your heart truly desires. Your gut feeling is the physical sensation that conveys messages from your intuition. Any task or behavior that feels meaningful to you will trigger a feeling of ecstasy, while tasks and behaviors that are harmful or provide no value will trigger anxiety, heart palpitations, migraines, and so on.

2. Observe When You Are Flowing

A state of flow is achieved when you lose a sense of time while performing a task. In that state of flow, you are creative, inspired, and content. Meaningful tasks and routines cause you to enter a state of flow and forget about everything else happening around you. These tasks may be associated with your career or your personal life. Incorporating some of these "flow activities" into your day can make each day feel meaningful.

3. Become Curious

It is impossible to find meaning when you are stuck in your comfort zone. You must be willing to ask questions, do trial and error, or explore new opportunities to connect to the things you find most significant. To practice having a curious mind, adopt a childlike attitude, and treat each experience as a learning opportunity. Even when performing mundane tasks, look for ways of becoming more efficient or creative in how you perform them. Deliberately create challenges for your brain so that you are forced to think differently.

4. Focus on Your Values

Your core values define what you stand for as an individual. Living a value-driven lifestyle can make each day feel meaningful because you are honoring the beliefs and principles that mean the most to you. In fact, living a value-driven lifestyle can lend itself to purpose since it offers you a sense of direction. Thus, by focusing on and prioritizing your values, you can achieve the quality of life you desire.

5. Find Someone to Love

Loving others is a form of selflessness. We do things for people without expecting anything done for us in return. However, the irony of selflessness is that by caring for others, it gives us a sense of responsibility, which makes us feel good about ourselves. Knowing that in some small or large way we are contributing to the well-being of others makes our lives feel deeply meaningful.

Therefore, even without finding your purpose, you can live in such a way that makes each day feel rewarding. All you need to do is figure out what feels meaningful to you, then incorporate those tasks or behaviors into your everyday life. As you explore and ask questions, your gut will lead you on the right path!

9

RETURN TO SPIRITUALITY

Spirituality is recognizing and celebrating that we are all inextricably connected to each other by a power greater than all of us, and that our connection to that power and to one another is grounded in love and compassion. Practicing spirituality brings a sense of perspective, meaning and purpose to our lives.
–Brené Brown

WHAT IS SPIRITUALITY?

Spirituality is a broad term that can be interpreted in different ways. In a general sense, spirituality is the ability to connect to a deeper aspect of who you are. This 'deeper aspect of you' could be your inner girl, consciousness or subconsciousness, or a Divine Being or entity.

The reason why it is important for you to connect to this deeper aspect of you is so you can have a broader and more encompassing understanding of life, and how you experience it. For example, one of the central themes of spirituality is searching for the meaning of life. It would be difficult for you to search for meaning while firmly rooted in what you already know. After all, if you knew the meaning of life, there wouldn't be a need to search for it.

Thus, to find meaning you need to seek beyond what you know

and be willing to let go of comfortable truths, in the hopes of finding higher truths that can positively enhance your quality of life. You may not even realize it, but throughout this book, you have been introduced to higher truths—truths that expand your knowledge of self and help you look at your life with fresh eyes. We could call this a spiritual experience because you have ventured into the unknown in hopes of finding answers beyond what you already know.

Spiritual experiences are often transcendental, meaning they are beyond the ordinary and push the limits of reality. Meditation can be considered a spiritual experience because it allows you to tap into your subconscious mind and bring forward ideas, thoughts, and emotions you wouldn't otherwise be able to connect with during an ordinary task. Another example of a spiritual experience is walking in nature. It is no coincidence that you gain deeper clarity when you are walking outdoors, especially when you are surrounded by greenery. You get to come as close as possible to the creative power of the universe that is experienced through nature, and this fills your mind and body with that same life-producing and nurturing energy.

Spiritually can, therefore, be summed up as the ability to connect to an entity or experience greater than yourself. And as a result of this connection, you are able to gain wisdom beyond your own human capacity, which can guide you on your healing path.

You can use mindfulness as a tool to shift your focus away from your outer life and toward your inner life. As you focus on your inner life, which includes your thoughts, emotions, and body sensations, you can gain a deeper awareness of the spiritual experience (beyond ordinary) that is taking place in that present moment.

HOW TO CONNECT TO YOUR HIGHER SELF

The concept of 'higher self' is a spiritual concept that refers to the part of you that hasn't been influenced by the ego. Other names used to describe the higher self are soul or spirit, and these words befitting since the higher self connects you to the Divine. This means that when you have tapped into your higher self, you are no longer constrained to your self-image, life story, or past trauma—you become the essence of your soul or spirit.

It might be easier to define the higher self by describing how you feel when this part of you is activated through transcendental practices, like meditation. When you are embodying your higher self, it can feel like you are temporarily out of your body, and subsequently are liberated from the cares of the body. Your mind no longer travels to the past or future since it is not confined to your life story, but instead travels deeper into your unconscious.

Due to the fact that your ego cannot access this Divine part of you, there is no inner resistance to truth. You accept and appreciate your existence and let go of any physical and psychic limitations. It is no wonder that many who are connected to their higher self are able to experience healing miracles or achieve phenomenal achievements in their lives. The absence of ego is what allows them to act from a place of 'being,' rather than a place of survival or fear.

Connecting to your higher self is also a valuable exercise when doing inner child work. Just imagine for a moment that you have access to Divine intelligence, and any question that arises in your mind is intuitively responded to. In essence, this is what occurs when you connect to your higher self. You discover that all along, you had answers to every question that you would ever ask, within you. And since the higher self is connected to the Divine, you can get answers to questions that are beyond your capacity of reasoning, such as finding your life purpose.

With access to so much spiritual power comes responsibility. While you have the built-in ability to commune with the Divine and gain knowledge and wisdom about your life, it is important to cultivate trust and patience (the two go hand-in-hand).

Firstly, you need to trust that there are higher truths that you are unaware of, and that by seeking these truths, you will find them. Secondly, you need to trust that God, ancestors, the universe, your inner girl, or whatever Divine entity you believe in, will always guide you toward the path you should go. In other words, trust that you are never lost because even the current life situation you are in is guiding you somewhere. Lastly, you need to trust your intuition, synchronici-ties, and whatever signs or symbols you are shown that convey messages only you can interpret. Divine intelligence won't always appear as a number, voice, text, or encounter with a human being. There are plenty of other ways you can discover and learn higher truths.

Once you have developed trust, patience will flow naturally. Instead of being desperate for answers, you will rest in the knowledge that whatever is meant for you will always reach you (this includes signs, assistance, revelations, etc.) Patience also makes the process of healing enjoyable because you are tuned into your day-to-day experi-ence, rather than waiting for that major "Aha" moment, which by the way is so rare. Coupled with the focus on your daily experiences is a deep sense of gratitude for the small changes you observe in your thinking, moods, and behaviors.

As you learn to trust that you are in the right place, at the right time, with the right intentions, and learn to be patient during your healing process, you will be able to connect to your inner girl and flow in whatever direction you are led.

Five Ways to Connect to Your Higher Self

When you are only aware of your physical self, healing is restricted to what your body can or cannot do, and your emotional life is heavily influenced by past experiences, emotional triggers, and the presence or lack of psychological tools like emotional regulation. But if you are fortunate enough to discover your spiritual self, you can transcend your physical experience, download higher truths that help you rede-fine your life, and inject your life with meaning.

There are many ways to connect to your higher self. If you have never had a transcendental experience before, you might feel uncom-fortable with the idea of having an out-of-body experience. But all an out-of-body experience means is playing the role of observer and exploring hidden parts of your inner life. It is important to do your research and find a transcendental practice that feels most comfortable to you. Below are five examples that you can consider:

1. Lucid Dreaming

The first transcendental practice happens naturally while you are sleeping. Your higher self can speak to you through dreams, during the stage of sleep known as rapid eye movement, or REM sleep. During REM sleep, your brain is active and working as though you were awake, however, your body is completely still. Lucid dreaming happens during this stage, and you are able to tap into your subconscious mind. Start a practice of recording your dreams when you wake up, noting the particular symbols and signs you were shown. Your dreams can expose hidden thoughts, desires, or emotions that were previously unconscious.

2. Higher Self Meditation

Another less invasive transcendental practice is meditation. Meditation can help you slow down your conscious mind so you can tap into your unconscious mind. Some of the best ways to relax your mind as you begin meditation is to focus on your breathing, taking slow and intentional breaths. You can also choose to focus on an object within view or think about a high-energy state like love, peace, or gratitude. As you think upon a high-energy state, you raise your awareness and break through the barrier of physical reality. This is when you are able to connect to your higher self and either enjoy the euphoria of being out of your body or pose questions and listen for answers.

3. Astral Projection

Astral projecting is the practice of leaving your physical body and entering a trance-like state. During astral projection, some people are able to feel their soul or spirit leaving their bodies, or they are able to watch their bodies as though they were a separate being observing it.

This experience can change your perception of who you are, as well as how you experience reality. Practicing a type of meditation known as hypnagogic mindfulness meditation can be the first step to practicing astral projection. Before or during your meditation, you can set an intention to connect to your higher self in that lucid state.

4. Journaling

Journaling is a great practice to use when seeking to connect with your higher self. However, not in the way you probably think. The common type of journaling is expressive writing, where you record the thoughts and emotions in your mind. This type of journaling won't allow you to have the out-of-body experience you are seeking. Instead, you will need to practice another type of journaling known as intuitive writing, where you write down immediate gut-reactions without giving yourself time to think about them. Afterward, you can go back and read what you wrote and determine which answers came from the ego and which came from your higher self. Ego answers are not necessarily bad, but they might be superficial or fear-based. Higher self answers are normally difficult to interpret at first due to the mind failing to process such profound wisdom, but over time the answers will make sense.

5. Imagination

Your neocortex and thalamus are two parts of the brain that are responsible for your imagination. They also happen to be responsible for abstract thought and consciousness. Your imagination might sometimes feel like made-up illusions, but it is important to note that these "illusions" come from your mind, meaning you have created them. You can connect to your higher self by imagining this part of you (similar to how you would imagine the inner girl), or remain open to receive inspiration from your higher self.

HOW TO AVOID THE EGO TRAP

As you return to spirituality, you will need to beware of the deceptive tricks of the ego. Before we move on to speak about the ego trap, I must remind you that the ego isn't a monster and that most of what comes across as self-sabotage, comes with good intentions. Your ego believes that it knows what's best for you based on your previous life experiences. It tries, by all means, to protect you from being faced with similar challenges from the past. Nonetheless, in its efforts to protect you, it can instill fear in your mind, or go the other way and make you see yourself as being larger than life itself.

The ego trap is an interesting experience. It often emerges along your spiritual journey, after you have come to certain realizations, such as being a spiritual being and believing that your life is more meaningful than present suffering. At this stage of your journey, you might celebrate, thinking that you have defeated the ego and all kinds of shadow traits, self-righteousness, or survival-based instincts. You might have even gained enough wisdom from your higher self, and inner girl, about your past that you believe your healing journey is complete.

This is usually when the trouble begins. Without living out spirituality on a daily basis, you rely on your theoretical understanding of spiritual concepts and shift from flowing in an open heart state to processing everything from a mental state. Slowly, and subtly, your ego starts to take over your life again, hiding behind religious dogma or a sense of moral superiority over others. The actual healing work can no longer continue until you have entered an ego trap.

There are a few telling signs that you have entered an ego trap:

- **You intellectualize spirituality.** Instead of connecting to your soul and seeking truth, you might memorize quotes from spiritual leaders, depend heavily on spiritual ideologies, and rationalize your spiritual experiences.
- **You have a need to be right about your spiritual views.** You may not take kindly to people challenging your spiritual

views, or even adopting different beliefs from you. You might even feel that it is your duty to 'educate' people on your spiritual views, so they can experience what you are experiencing. Your 'truth' is treated as the whole truth and every other discovery is seen as being wrong or false.

- **You see spiritual development as a hierarchy.** When you look at other people, you might feel more spiritually advanced or superior than they are. This idea may cause you to judge those who are less spiritual than you.

- **You are afraid of experiencing negative emotions.** You might believe that being spiritual means always being positive. However, this isn't realistic. While you are a spiritual being, you still reside in a physical body and, therefore, aren't immune to shadow traits. It isn't fair on yourself to put on a positive look and deny your negative emotions because they carry messages too.

- **You have a savior complex.** You might believe that it is your responsibility to save the world and take on other people's burdens since you were able to heal from your painful past. As noble as it is to be of service to other people, it is wise to know your physical limits and draw boundaries. Once again, you might be wise beyond your years, but you cannot alleviate the suffering from others. Just as you were able to humble yourself to the Divine, your loved ones and colleagues must choose to go on that journey on their own, and experience the same freedom you have.

Don't feel bad if you slip and find yourself in an ego trap. It is a common experience among those who are spiritually enlightened. The best way to get yourself out of the trap is to reconnect with your heart and find out what made you shut down, or switch from feeling your way through to thinking your way through.

Practice Ego Relaxation

In order to get on a spiritual path, you need to surrender what you know (or think you know) and seek higher truths. Taking this action can bruise your ego because letting go of what you know is a form of ego death. Since the ego likes to be in control, you might find it difficult to willingly surrender and allow yourself to deepen your spiritual awareness.

Due to the amount of internal resistance that can come with spiritual ascendance, one way to manage the ego is by practicing ego relaxation. Instead of abandoning the ego and having to face inner discomfort, you can lean toward the ego and envelope it with compassion, validation, and mercy.

Think of the ego as being akin to a block of ice. There are two ways to deconstruct the ice: You can either pick up a hammer and smash it into small pieces or simply allow the cube to melt into a puddle of water. The latter is the path of least resistance.

When dealing with your ego, it is important to handle it with care. The ego is already hyper-sensitive, but more than that, it is still a part of who you are. If you treat it unkindly, understand that you are causing suffering for yourself. Therefore, taking the path of least resistance is the loving approach to minimizing the role and influence of your ego while you travel on your spiritual journey.

How would ego relaxation look in real life? Let's say you are at work and due to a stressful situation react with an old behavioral pattern. Afterward, you feel a strong inclination to beat yourself up or 'correct' your behavior since you are no longer the aggressive woman you used to be. In that moment, instead of beating yourself up, you could simply sit with your feelings of guilt, or whatever emerges from the shadow, and refrain from causing any more hurt. You could even whisper to yourself:

- There is nothing I need to do.
- There is nothing I need to say.
- There is nowhere I need to go.
- There is nothing I need to understand.
- There is nothing more that needs to happen.

As your body's defenses relax, so, too, will the ego. And instead of being made to feel like a monster, your ego will learn that triggers are met with patience, love, and compassion. Thus, ego relaxation is about resisting the urge to react or travel to the past or future. You resist the negative beliefs about yourself or others that might seek to distort what is actually taking place in the present moment. You choose to stay right where you are and face whatever you need to face, without having to defend yourself.

Ego relaxation is a valuable exercise, not only when seeking to stay connected to your higher self, but also when the shadow emerges and attempts to take over your personality. Instead of punishing yourself for exhibiting what you consider bad qualities, you can lean toward those qualities and show compassion. A wonderful Zen koan that captures the experience of ego relaxation goes: *"Be nothing, do nothing, get nothing, become nothing, seek for nothing, relinquish nothing. Be as you are. Rest in God"* (Macpherson, 2018).

Relaxing the ego and recentering yourself in the present moment is a form of love. You choose to love the chaotic or triggered parts of you, rather than punishing yourself for feeling or overreacting. Of course, this can only be done when you are connected to your higher self because judgment and self-criticism are signs of identification with the body.

Flowing in this state of love is healing and deeply nurturing for the inner girl. You show her, through your loving actions, that you accept the good, bad, and ugly of who she is. The final chapter will explore what it means to practice self-love, and how you can offer yourself the safety and nurturing you didn't receive as a child.

10

RETURN TO LOVE

As I began to love myself, I recognized that my mind can disturb me and it can make me sick. But as I connected it to my heart, my mind became a valuable ally. Today I call this connection "WISDOM OF THE HEART"
–Charlie Chaplin

HEAL THE INNER VOID WITH LOVE

We have reached the final chapter of the book, and where we are closing looks and feels different from where we started. Perhaps this is symbolic of your personal journey through reading this book—you are not the same person in Chapter 10 as you were in Chapter 1. In just a short space of time, you have stretched your mind tremendously and gotten the opportunity to see who you could be if only you would heal your inner girl.

It is no coincidence that this last chapter is based on love, more particularly the love you show yourself. Yes, loving others is important, but cannot be done without first loving who you are. The two conditions are inextricably linked. As quoted in the Gospel of Luke in the Bible: *"How can you say to your brother, 'Brother, let me take the speck out of your eye,' when you yourself fail to see the plank in your own eye?"* (Luke 6:42 NIV).

The same can be said about self-love and how it relates to the love you show others: How can you say you genuinely love others when it is so difficult for you to show yourself love? Therefore, it is more appropriate for us to explore the concept of self-love and allow brotherly love to follow suit naturally.

The topic of self-love may be a hard one for you to think about, especially if you had an insecure attachment with your parents. One of your main needs as a little girl was safety, but only because security was a form of love. In your fragile state, having someone who could soothe you when you were crying, cuddle you until you slept, or reaffirmed their acceptance and unconditional love was the best way for you to feel loved and secure.

The lack of safety meant that you grew up not really understanding what love was, or at least having a perverted understanding of love. For instance, if your parents expected you to perform a certain way in order to validate you, you may have learned that being loved involves sacrificing your individuality and personal quirks. Alternatively, if you were raised by parents who were narcissistic and demanded most of the attention in the home, then you may have learned that love comes at the cost of having your own needs pushed to the side.

The unhealthy dynamics you learned at home, influenced your understanding of love and ability to show and receive love. As a spiritual being who flourishes at the energetic frequency of love, not being comfortable showing or receiving love has created an inner void. The inner void is that feeling of emptiness that may be connected with feelings of despair, loneliness, or depression. The emptiness has a lot to do with unmet emotional needs that your inner girl still yearns for, hence the despair or loneliness. Trying to mask this inner void each day only prolongs the suffering. The antidote can only be filling the void with self-love.

BE THE PARENT YOU NEVER HAD

When you experience a childhood emotional wound, a part of your soul dies. With each repeated loss or trauma, you begin to retreat from others even more and eventually hide from yourself too. In this trauma-induced state, you are likely to fit on a mask and show up as who others expect you to be, rather than the bubbly, free-spirited, and outspoken person you once were. You might live like this for a month or two, although if your trauma is left unaddressed, this can become how you show yourself to the world.

Many adults who experienced childhood trauma are estranged from themselves and have either forgotten or denied who they are. As a result, cultivating self-love seems like an impossible task because they are disconnected from self. It is as though the wounded inner child is trapped in a self-built prison and won't be allowed to speak up and receive the healing it deserves. Of course, the addict within flourishes in this state and can worsen an already devastating existential crisis!

Since showing yourself love can sometimes be difficult during trauma healing, it can be a good approach to take the role of a parent and retrain yourself on how to think and feel based on empowering beliefs and values. In psychology, this therapeutic practice is known as reparenting. With reparenting, you are given the opportunity to step outside your shoes and become a parental figure that provides your inner girl with the psychological needs she didn't receive from her original parents. It doesn't matter whether you become her mother or father, what matters is the positive role you play.

If you have never been a parent before, don't worry. What your inner girl needs is what you already have within you! This may not seem apparent right now, but as soon as you start listening and responding to your inner girl's needs, you will realize that the love, validation, or acceptance she needs were emotions you already had the capacity to give. In other words, just because you never received love as a child, doesn't mean you don't know what love is like. Sure, you may need to practice showing love to yourself, but you are capable of addressing this emotional need.

There are generally four skills that children raised with insecure attachments aren't taught during childhood. These skills include:

- **Love and respect:** Parents are supposed to teach their kids how to respect others, as well as themselves. This might include teaching centered around language, boundaries, and morals. Parents are also meant to show their children how to be compassionate toward others and practice self-love.
- **Self-belief and self-confidence:** Through positive reinforcement and emotional validation, parents are supposed to help their kids develop a healthy self-esteem, help them believe in their talents and abilities, and show them how to bounce back after setbacks.
- **Emotional management:** Parents are responsible for modeling self-control and teaching their children how to regulate their emotions, resolve conflict, and cope with stress and anxiety.
- **Communication skills:** It is also the responsibility of parents to teach their children how to converse with other people, both in informal and formal environments, as well as how to recognize non-verbal cues and body language.

Even though you cannot turn back time and change how you were raised, you can become the parent you needed as a child. Take the time to regularly check in on your inner girl, and see how she's doing, and how she is feeling. Use positive and affirming language, even if it sounds uncomfortable at first. When you speak to your inner girl, use a gentle and warm tone of voice so you can gradually re-program the sound of your inner voice. For example, after a while, your inner voice won't sound as aggressive as your original parent, but will be calmer and more patient with you.

Reparenting yourself isn't only supposed to be used when healing your inner girl. You can also use it as a way to make new memories with your inner girl. For example, once every month, you can ask your inner girl where she would like to visit and plan a trip to that location. It could be a theme park, arcade, restaurant, or the cinema (depending on how old your inner girl is). You can choose to go alone or ask a friend to accompany you (somebody that your inner girl enjoys being around too). These types of fun excursions can help you create positive memories to replace your old childhood memories.

Lastly, reparenting affirmations can also be a great tool to use when seeking to imprint new beliefs about who you are. Every morning or evening, you can recite these affirmations while looking in the mirror and take the time to pause and really think about each one before moving to the next.

Make Your Inner Voice an Ally

How you speak to yourself has a lot to do with how you were spoken to as a child. However, your self-talk tends to be biased toward the negative messages you received, rather than the positive affirmation. This is due to how the brain processes negative and positive information; that is, you are more likely to attend to, and dwell on negative stimuli more than positive stimuli.

In essence, even if your parents gave you plenty of praise, you are more likely to recall, more vividly, times when they criticized you. The 5:1 praise to criticism ratio is used in psychology to help parents nurture their children's self-esteem. For every criticism, parents are encouraged to praise their children five times. As a surrogate parent to your inner girl, you can use the 5:1 ratio to positively change your self-talk and make your inner voice an ally. Below are other scientific techniques that can improve how you speak to yourself:

1. Say "Stop!"

After you catch yourself entertaining a negative thought, immediately shout "Stop!" Researchers have found that doing this can help you manage stress and anxiety, improve the quality of your sleep, and control overthinking. After saying "Stop!" you also get a moment of pause where you can practice mindfulness or check on your behavior, then proceed with a more helpful thought.

2. Ask Yourself Questions

In a study on introspective self-talk, researchers found that participants who asked themselves questions were able to solve more problems than those who made statements that they would succeed (Senay et al., 2010). One explanation for this is that the brain works harder when it is given a challenge, which can enhance creativity and learning. Asking questions also means venturing into the unknown and not relying on preconceived ideas and beliefs. You are likely to maintain a positive mindset when you are showing curiosity and are open to learning new things.

3. "You" Versus "I"

Speaking about yourself in second-person, such as using the word "You," can make you feel more confident. In a study, stressed participants were asked to give a public speech in front of judges in a competition to win their dream job. Half of the participants were told to speak about themselves in first-person using "I" and the other half were told to speak about themselves in second-person using "You," or their name. Those who used "You" or their name when addressing themselves reported feeling less nervous and more confident. Moreover, the judges also viewed them more favorably than those who spoke in first-person (Kross et al., 2014).

4. Give Yourself Clear Instructions to Follow

Instead of commenting on your performance or setting high expectations, give yourself clear instructions to follow. Doing this not only helps you maintain focus but also helps you become action-oriented. You can see how much progress you have made and how far you still need to go. Giving yourself instructions can also help you separate who you are from what you do. For example, if you are unable to complete all of your daily tasks, the issue becomes about time management or preparation and planning, rather than evidence of personal inadequacy.

5. Use Energizing Language

Words carry energy. If you don't believe it, assess how differently you feel when you repeat the words 'tired' and 'happy' over and over again. Energizing language, such as telling yourself "I am proud of you" can uplift your mood and help you build inner resilience. More-over, it can also help you regulate your emotions and cope during stressful times.

6. Surround Yourself With Positive People

While there are many factors about your environment that you cannot control, who you surround yourself with isn't one of them. You get to choose the people who form part of your community, and those who you allow into your inner circle. Choosing to be around positive people can influence your own mental and emotional states. Plus, since one person's energy can rub on another, being around positive people can make you feel encouraged. Assess how you feel when you are around specific people, and how your mood changes as soon as you leave their company. If you are constantly walking away feeling drained, that could become detrimental to your own mental and emotional well-being.

It matters how you speak to yourself because your inner girl is always listening. As much as you confess to loving her, do your words and thoughts convey this love? This is a deep question to reflect on, perhaps during a time of meditation. Nevertheless, what is true is that your inner girl responds positively to both acts and words of affirmation.

Returning to love and learning how to practice self-love is a journey on its own. You are not expected to get it right on the first, second, or third attempt. In some cases, it could take years, and many back-and-forth experiences before you can develop a healthy self-esteem, accept yourself as you are, and treat yourself with love and compassion.

CONCLUSION

This book wasn't your typical addiction book, was it? Even though we touched on the cause and symptoms of chemical and behavioral addictions, that wasn't the focus. The purpose of this book was to show you how childhood pain, loss, and trauma could potentially lead you to the point of developing an addiction.

By the time the excessive drinker or eater discovers they have an addiction, the addict within has already formed, and is governing their life with an iron fist. Nothing is as ruthless and unforgiving as the addict within, who seeks to numb, deny, or mask trauma at all costs. The addict becomes a prisoner in their own body, feeling too ashamed to cry out for help, even though they need it.

As Jung rightly pointed out, all the addict seeks is a sense of wholeness. Unfortunately, the reluctance to confront their emotional distress causes addicts to turn to maladaptive behaviors that lead to bondage. If only we can learn from the addict's experience and find the courage within ourselves to heal, perhaps we will be fortunate enough to experience this sense of wholeness that comes from being aligned with who we are.

To prevent life-threatening addictions, you must stop the addict within from taking over your life. The best way to do this is to travel where you are too afraid to go—back to the past. Even though you cannot restore the past, you can gain wisdom from it and provide yourself the healing you deserve.

Inner girl work can help you heal from childhood emotional wounds that haven't yet been resolved. By connecting to this aspect of your subconscious mind, you are able to access memories, thoughts, beliefs, and emotions that have been suppressed for many years. As uncomfortable as it may be recalling the pain you had to endure as a little girl, you can finally mourn the loss of what you were unable to receive.

Your inner girl has been calling out for you, and now you are in the position to respond to her. The bond you share can become what inspires you to redefine who you are, and it cultivates the kind of relationships and life experiences you were never given or exposed to as a child. No longer do you need to wait on anyone to provide for you what you can provide for yourself.

You have been given the tools to heal your psyche and body from unaddressed trauma. And even greater than this, you have been shown the path to spiritual enlightenment. With the tools you have been given, and the access to your higher self, you have the power to turn your life around. So, what is it going to be? Are you going to choose to heal the addict within?

As a token of gratitude for exploring this book, claim your complimentary 'Unlock Your Inner Girl Affirmations Deck' by visiting: https://BookHip.com/LQDTWAS

ACKNOWLEDGMENTS

I extend my profound gratitude to the individuals whose unwavering support and guidance have been instrumental in bringing this book to life:

• **My Family:** For their enduring love, unwavering encouragement, and steadfast belief in me, even during moments of self-doubt.

• **Lolo:** For her expertise in navigating the complexities of addiction and thought patterns. Her invaluable insights have greatly enriched the content of this book.

• **Barbie:** For her constant support, understanding, and encouragement. She has been a beacon of inspiration and motivation throughout this journey. Special thanks also to CJ and Hayley for their support during challenging times.

• **Nyasha:** For his dedication and commitment to providing resources and support whenever needed. His tireless efforts in shaping and refining this manuscript have been truly invaluable.

• **To the Readers:** I am deeply grateful for your openness, courage, and willingness to explore the depths of your inner landscapes. Your engagement fuels my passion for writing and sharing transformative messages.

From the bottom of my heart, thank you.

REFERENCES

AACAP. (2019, May). *Alcohol use in families*. Aacap.org. https://www.aacap.org/AACAP/ Families_and_Youth/Facts_for_Families/FFF-Guide/Children-Of-Alcoholics-017.aspx

Addenbrooke, M. (n.d.). *Jung and the labyrinth of addiction*. Society of Analytical Psychology. https://www.thesap.org.uk/articles-on-jungian-psychology-2/about-analysis-and-therapy/jung-and-the-labyrinth-of-addiction/

Adey, O. (2022, January 31). *Psychology: According to expert, there are 7 archetypes of the inner child - which one are you?* Get to Text. https://gettotext.com/psychology-according-to-expert-there-are-7-archetypes-of-the-inner-child-which-one-are-you/

Aiyana, S. (2020, January 4). *How to do inner child work for healing trauma and self-acceptance*. Rising Woman. https://risingwoman.com/inner-child-work-healing-trauma-self-acceptance/

Alavi, S. S., Ferdosi, M., Jannatifard, F., Eslami, M., Alaghemandan, H., & Setare, M. (2012). Behavioral addiction versus substance addiction: Correspondence of psychiatric and psychological views. *International Journal of Preventive Medicine*, 3(4), 290–294. https://www.ncbi.nlm.nih.gov/pmc/articles/PMC3354400/

Alexander, B. (2015, July 23). *The spiritual ego trap*. Spirituality & Health. https://www.spiritualityhealth.com/blogs/conscious-living/2015/07/23/bianca-alexander-spiritual-ego-trap

Ana-Maria. (2021, March 22). *The 5 "wounded" inner child archetypes — Which archetype are you?* Luna Voda Coaching. https://lunavoda.com/the-5-wounded-inner-child-archetypes-which-archetype-are-you/

Beauty After Bruises. (2019, January 25). *Self-care 101: Featuring 101 self-care techniques for trauma survivors*. Beauty after Bruises. https://www.beautyafterbruises.org/blog/selfcare

Blackford, M. (2018, October 9). *Behavioral addiction vs. Drug addiction - What's the difference?* FHE Health. https://fherehab.com/learning/difference-beahvioral-drug-addiction

REFERENCES

Brady, K. (2019, June 5). *5 Types of boundaries for your relationship*. Keir Brady Counseling Services. https://keirbradycounseling.com/relationship-boundaries/

Channel Islands Rehab. (2020, February 19). *Obsession vs Addiction: What's the difference?* Channel Islands Rehab. https://channelislandsrehab.com/obsession-vs-addiction-whats-the-difference/

Cherry, K. (2020, December 11). *Individualistic cultures and behavior*. Verywell Mind. https://www.verywellmind.com/what-are-individualistic-cultures-2795273

Cherry, K. (2022, February 14). *What is self-concept and how does it form?* Verywell Mind. https://www.verywellmind.com/what-is-self-concept-2795865

Chi, T. (2017, April 28). *Is addiction a mental illness?* Talkspace. https://www.talkspace.com/blog/addiction-mental-illness/

Crane, M. (2021, September 29). *What are the traits of an addictive personality?* American Addiction Centers. https://americanaddictioncenters.org/the-addiction-cycle/traits-of-an-addictive-personality

Crawford, M. J., & Prince, M. (1999). Increasing rates of suicide in young men in England during the 1980s: the importance of social context. *Social Science & Medicine*, *49*(10), 1419–1423. https://doi.org/10.1016/s0277-9536(99)00213-0

Davis, S. (2020a, July 13). *The wounded inner child*. CPTSD Foundation. https://cptsdfoundation.org/2020/07/13/the-wounded-inner-child/

Davis, S. (2020b, July 27). *Reparenting to heal the wounded inner child*. CPTSD Foundation. https://cptsdfoundation.org/2020/07/27/reparenting-to-heal-the-wounded-inner-child/

Delagran, L. (2019). *What is spirituality?* Taking Charge of Your Health & Wellbeing. https://www.takingcharge.csh.umn.edu/what-spirituality

Facing History and Ourselves. (2019). *Individual and society*. Facing History and Ourselves. https://www.facinghistory.org/holocaust-and-human-behavior/chapter-1/introduction

Fairyington, S. (2022, February 23). *Connecting to your higher self will transform your life*. Oprah Daily. https://www.oprahdaily.com/life/health/a38736167/how-to-connect-to-your-higher-self/

Farlex Dictionary of Idioms. (2015). *Too much of a good thing*. TheFreeDictionary.com. https://idioms.thefreedictionary.com/too+much+of+a+good+thing

Florida Tech. (2018, June 28). *The importance of attachment in early child development*. Florida Tech Online. https://www.floridatechonline.com/blog/psychology/the-importance-of-attachment-in-early-child-development/

Gateway Foundation. (2019, December 2). *Why trauma often leads to addiction*. Gateway. https://www.gatewayfoundation.org/addiction-blog/trauma-and-addiction/

Glordano, A. L. (2021, July 28). *Is emotion regulation the key to addiction prevention?* Www.psychologytoday.com. https://www.psychologytoday.com/us/blog/understanding-addiction/202107/is-emotion-regulation-the-key-addiction-prevention

Goldstein, E. (n.d.). *What is an inner child and what does it know*. Integrative Psychotherapy and Trauma Treatment. https://integrativepsych.co/new-blog/what-is-an-inner-child

Good Reads. (n.d.-a). *A quote by Jiddu Krishnamurti*. Www.goodreads.com. https://www.goodreads.com/quotes/13620-it-is-no-measure-of-health-to-be-well-adjusted#:~:text=Quotes%20%3E%20Quotable%20Quote-

Good Reads. (n.d.-b). *Addiction quotes (1269 quotes)*. Www.goodreads.com. https://www.goodreads.com/quotes/tag/addiction

Good Reads. (n.d.-c). *Brené Brown quote*. Www.goodreads.com. https://www.goodreads.com/author/show/162578.Bren_Brown

Good Reads. (n.d.-d). *Charlie Chaplin quote*. Www.goodreads.com. https://www.goodreads.com/author/show/48136.Charlie_Chaplin

Good Reads. (n.d.-e). *Craig D. Lounsbrough quote*. Www.goodreads.com. https://www.goodreads.com/author/show/4172966.Craig_D_Lounsbrough

Good Reads. (n.d.-f). *Glennon Doyle quote*. Www.goodreads.com. https://www.goodreads.com/author/show/17099759.Glennon_Doyle

Good Reads. (n.d.-g). *Inner child quotes (99 quotes)*. Www.goodreads.com. https://www.goodreads.com/quotes/tag/inner-child?page=2

Good Reads. (n.d.-h). *Steve Maraboli quote*. Www.goodreads.com. https://www.goodreads.com/author/show/4491185.Steve_Maraboli

REFERENCES

Good Reads. (2019). *Yukio Mishima quote.* Goodreads.com. https://www.goodreads.com/author/show/35258.Yukio_Mishima

Gurteen, D. (2018, April 2). *What is a real community?* Conversational Leadership. https://conversational-leadership.net/community/

Harvey, C. (2019, September 20). *The way we speak to our children becomes their inner voice.* Kurtz Psychology. https://www.kurtzpsychology.com/the-way-we-speak-to-our-children-becomes-their-inner-voice/

Hopeful Panda. (2022, February 25). *Inner child work: 10 Ways on how to connect with your inner child.* Hopeful Panda. https://hopefulpanda.com/inner-child/

InnerDrive. (n.d.). *6 Ways to improve how you talk to yourself.* Blog.innerdrive.co.uk. https://blog.innerdrive.co.uk/6-ways-to-improve-how-you-talk-to-yourself

Klammer, S. (n.d.). *Inner child drawings.* Expressive Art Workshops. https://www.expressiveartworkshops.com/expressive-art-e-courses/30-day-expressive-drawing-challenges/inner-child-drawings/

Krause, C. (2017, July 26). *Following your inner child to your life's purpose.* Elephant Journal. https://www.elephantjournal.com/2017/07/following-your-inner-child-to-your-lifes-purpose/

Kross, E., Bruehlman-Senecal, E., Park, J., Burson, A., Dougherty, A., Shablack, H., Bremner, R., Moser, J., & Ayduk, O. (2014). Self-talk as a regulatory mechanism: How you do it matters. *Journal of Personality and Social Psychology, 106*(2), 304–324. https://doi.org/10.1037/a0035173

Leobart. (2020, February 24). *11 Bukowski quotes on life and death.* Medium. https://medium.com/@leobartwrites/11-bukowski-quotes-on-life-and-death-89318fa44302#:~:text=%E2%80%9CWhat%20is%20terrible%20is%20not

Lumen Learning. (n.d.). *8.1 Foundations of culture and identity.* Courses.lumenlearning.com. https://courses.lumenlearning.com/suny-realworldcomm/chapter/8-1-foundations-of-culture-and-identity/

Lynch, E. (n.d.). *Evanna Lynch quote.* Www.goodreads.com. https://www.goodreads.com/author/show/7255387.Evanna_Lynch

REFERENCES

Macpherson, M. (2018). *Surrender: The practice of ego relaxation.* Kripalu. https://kripalu. org/resources/surrender-practice-ego-relaxation

Manning, M. (2021, May 2). *Ask for help!* Medium. https://psiloveyou.xyz/ask-for-help-b7146dc89e5

Merriam-Webster. (2018). *Definition of addict.* Merriam-Webster.com. https://www. merriam-webster.com/dictionary/addict

Mountain Vista Farm. (n.d.). *Red flags for addiction in others.* Mountain Vista Farm. https://mountainvistafarm.com/help-now/red-flags/

N, M. V. (2021, January 15). *Can't find your purpose in life?* Illumination Curated. https:// medium.com/illumination-curated/cant-find-your-purpose-in-life-53e1cba2d0ce

National Institute on Drug Abuse. (2020, July). *Drugs and the brain.* National Institute on Drug Abuse. https://nida.nih.gov/publications/drugs-brains-behavior-science-addic tion/drugs-brain

Othon, J. E. (2017, October 20). *Carl Jung and the shadow: The ultimate guide to the human dark side.* HighExistence. https://highexistence.com/carl-jung-shadow-guide-unconscious/

Pikorn, I. (2019, August 30). *Noticing, healing and freeing your inner child.* Insight Timer Blog. https://insighttimer.com/blog/inner-child-meaning-noticing-healing-freeing/#: ~:text=In%20popular%20psychology%2C%20the%20inner

Project Helping. (2018, June 7). *Physical, mental, and emotional self care – Part 2.* Project Helping. https://projecthelping.org/self-care-2/#:~:text=Some%20easy%20ways%20to%20relax,it%20makes%20you%20feel%20relaxed!

Quercus. (2017, October 9). *Topic: How to build a support network.* Www.beyondblue.org.au. https://www.beyondblue.org.au/get-support/online-forums/staying-well/how-to-build-a-support-network

Quinn, J. (2020, June 7). *How to do shadow work and reclaim your authenticity.* Consciousness Liberty. https://consciousnessliberty.com/how-to-do-shadow-work-reclaim-your-authenticity/

Raypole, C. (2020, February 28). *Types of addiction and how they're treated.* Healthline. https://www.healthline.com/health/types-of-addiction#behavioral

REFERENCES

Regan, S. (2022, February 27). *A quick practice for relieving stress and tension — Anytime, anywhere.* Mindbodygreen. https://www.mindbodygreen.com/articles/body-scan-meditation-how-it-works-benefits-tips-more#:~:text=Connecting%20to%20your%20body&text=In%20fact%2C%20research%20shows%20that

Robins, A. (2020, April 12). *Healing and recovery for daughters of narcissistic mothers.* Amanda Robins Psychotherapy. https://www.amandarobinspsychotherapy.com.au/articles/inner-child-art-therapy

Senay, I., Albarracín, D., & Noguchi, K. (2010). Motivating goal-directed behavior through introspective self-talk. *Psychological Science, 21*(4), 499–504. https://doi.org/10.1177/0956797610364751

Smith, J. A. (2018, January 10). *How to find your purpose in life.* Greater Good. https://greatergood.berkeley.edu/article/item/how_to_find_your_purpose_in_life

Sol, M. (2022, April 29). *Shadow self: How to embrace your inner darkness (3 techniques).* Loner Wolf. https://lonerwolf.com/shadow-self/#13_types_of_shadow_self

Thurmond, N. (2015, February 21). *Healing from trauma and setting boundaries in relationships.* Eating Disorder Hope. https://www.eatingdisorderhope.com/treatment-for-eating-disorders/co-occurring-dual-diagnosis/trauma-ptsd/healing-from-trauma-and-setting-boundaries-in-relationships

Tull, M. (2020, December 14). How to use journaling to cope with PTSD. *Verywell Mind.* https://www.verywellmind.com/how-to-use-journaling-to-cope-with-ptsd-2797594#:~:text=Begin%20writing%20about%20your%20deepest

Tuttle, C. (2019, October 2). *Are you profiling your wounded self? 9 Questions to help you find out.* Live Your Truth. https://my.liveyourtruth.com/dyt/are-you-profiling-your-wounded-self/

Whitley, R. (2017, July 28). *Is an increase in individualism damaging our mental health?* Www.psychologytoday.com. https://www.psychologytoday.com/us/blog/talking-about-men/201707/is-increase-in-individualism-damaging-our-mental-health

Wiedmann, F. (2018, October 29). *Searching for your purpose? Ask your inner child.* Www.blinkist.com. https://www.blinkist.com/magazine/posts/searching-purpose-ask-inner-child

REFERENCES

Wood, K. (2022, March 17). *What is the purpose of life and how to find purpose in life.* Lifehack. https://www.lifehack.org/articles/lifestyle/how-find-your-lifes-purpose-and-make-yourself-better-person.html

Yugay, I. (2022, May 10). *How to connect with your higher self, according to spirituality teachers.* Mindvalley Blog. https://blog.mindvalley.com/higher-self/

ABOUT THE AUTHOR

Meet Anne Lunar, an exceptional individual whose wealth of knowledge and boundless compassion knows no limits. Her diverse education background spans fields such as Psychology, Health, Domestic Violence, Law Enforcement, Business, Design, Fashion and the Building Industry. Anne's journey has been one of continuous growth and exploration.

With over 29 years of expertise in human health, well-being, and safety, especially with females and children, Anne has become a beacon of hope for those seeking solace and support. Her unwavering commitment to helping others and her belief in individual betterment has driven her to embark on a mission to spread healing and positivity.

Anne's life experiences have revealed a profound truth: we are all interconnected and capable of inspiring each other, especially during moments of despair. In a world that sometimes seems divided, Anne's stories and teachings remind us of our shared humanity and the incredible capacity we possess to heal and uplift each other.

Currently, Anne is pouring her heart and soul into creating an intriguing sequel in progress for the Healing from Within Series. These books promise to inspire and empower those seeking growth and healing.

Anne Lunar's journey is one of continuous evolution—a quest to improve herself and those around her. Her warmth, compassion, and wisdom make her an author whose work is not only enlightening but also profoundly touching.

Made in the USA
Monee, IL
22 November 2024

70911026R00077